COLUMBIA

ooksack

Skagit

Sauk-Suiattle

attle

CASCADE MOUNTAINS

TAHOMA

MOUNT RAINIER

SYLVAN

PUGET SOUND AND SOME OF THE TRIBES OF NORTHWEST WASHINGTON

NISQUALLY WATERSHED

MAP AREA

Yakama

MESSAGES FROM FRANK'S LANDING

Also by Charles Wilkinson

Messages from Frank's Landing

A STORY OF SALMON,

TREATIES, AND THE

INDIAN WAY

CHARLES WILKINSON

Photo essay by Hank Adams
Maps by Diane Sylvain

UNIVERSITY OF WASHINGTON PRESS
Seattle & London

Dedicated to

Professor RALPH W. JOHNSON

*who heard the messages from Frank's Landing
and took them into his mind and heart*

The evergreen stand on Medicine Creek in 1854 has left a lone witness to history. The resilient Treaty Tree maintains its watch on the western edge of the Nisqually River delta.

CONTENTS

MESSAGES FROM FRANK'S LANDING

INTRODUCTION: 1945

After the family dinner, Billy Frank, Jr., walked out into the chilly December air and down to the bank of the Nisqually River. The fourteen-year-old boy shoved the canoe, a carved out cross-section of a cedar log, into the water. He poled the canoe upstream from a standing position, knowing the river, unhindered by the darkness. Besides, it had to be dark. The state game wardens were cracking down on Indian fishermen. They knew that Billy fished this stretch of water.

He made his way half a mile up the river, passing under the old Pacific Highway bridge to the eddy just beyond it. During the past few days he had made his repairs to the fifty-foot cotton net stowed in the canoe. "My dad always told me to prepare for the salmon coming back. Don't get caught in a hurry. Have it done in advance. He told me about a guy cutting a net in the dark and stabbing himself in the stomach. 'Don't be like that,' he told me." Billy unwrapped the net and set it neatly, with the corks on the top keeping the apparatus afloat and the weights on the other side of the net resting on the river bottom.

With the net in place, the boy lashed the canoe to the limbs of a fallen maple tree overhanging the eddy. "It was like a tunnel under there. And the canoe looks just like a log. There's no way they could see it." His work done, he strode back to his home at Frank's Landing on the riverside trail that cut through the tangle of vine maple, ferns, and blackberry.

He knew the way by heart. "We didn't walk on the roads. All we walked were trails. Indians have always used that river trail. It went all the way up to our mountain."

He was up early the next morning, still needing the dark. He made his way back up the trail. The net had done its work, taking some steelhead and a load of chum salmon. This was the renowned late chum run bound for Muck Creek. "I knew they'd be there because Muck Creek had just sent down the big winter freshet that gets the salmon going every year. And that downed maple hanging out over the eddy would give them shade and shelter." He would sell his catch to nearby farmers, who would like this fresh meat.

Billy laid the fish in the canoe, then folded the net and stowed it. He poled out into the current, floated under the bridge, and headed toward the gravel bar on the far side of the river. The bar was a good place to butcher the fish. He unloaded his fish and went to work, the gravel rasping his knees through the rubber hip boots. Take off the head, the fins, the tail with the sharp knife. Draw the knife up along the backbone. Make the fillets in the old way. Quick and efficient, but neat and respectful.

The two flashlights hit him dead on, no more than fifty feet away: "YOU'RE UNDER ARREST!"

Billy jumped to his feet and scrambled frantically across the bar toward the brush, awkward in his hip boots. At the edge of the brush he stumbled and fell. The two game wardens were on him and had him by the arms.

"Leave me alone, god*dam* it," the struggling boy screamed out, "I *fish* here! *I LIVE HERE!*"

This incident, just before Christmas of 1945, marked the first of more than fifty arrests that Billy Frank, Jr., would endure over the course of three decades. The moment coincided with the beginning of the post–World War II boom that jump-started the economy of Seattle, Puget Sound, and the Pacific Northwest, changing forever the lands and waters and, particularly for Billy, the river that rushes through his veins. Almost incredibly, he became a principal figure in those sweeping events, first as a warrior for his people's rights and their river, then as a statesman, bringing people together by dint of his charisma and his genius for gauging the public will and the interests of constituency groups.

Yet, for all his rare personal skills, Billy stands for something much larger. His eyes and soul have borne witness, not just to the epic events since 1945 and to the times since his birth in 1931, but also to a long line of human experiences stretching back immeasurably far before then. Billy's father, a skilled practitioner of the Indian oral tradition who lived for

Police assaults against Indian fishing once were routine. Tear gassed, Michael Hunt was among 62 arrested in a 1970 incident that prompted filing of a federal lawsuit to protect treaty rights.

more than a century, painted vivid word pictures of what he had seen.

"My dad was a great storyteller. He was always telling me stories. I can't explain what it's like to have your parents around so long. It's a very powerful thing to have your dad live to be a hundred and four. Mom lived almost that long herself. You've got to have someone who holds us together, who keeps us strong. Mom and Dad did that. You'd think: 'They'll be here tomorrow.'

"I had coffee with them in their house every morning of my adult life, every day I was in town. Dad had a shaving brush and one of those mugs. I'd go over every Saturday morning and shave him with one of those.

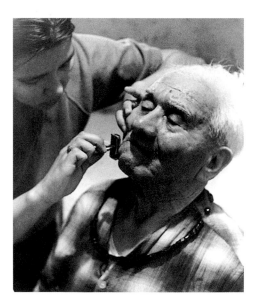

Born in 1879, Willie Frank devoted his life to the welfare of Nisqually Indians. In a pleasure of shared moments, Suzette Mills shaves her grandfather at his Frank's Landing home.

We'd all do it. Al and Maiselle, Suzette, Alison. That's not a big thing but it *is* a big thing. He probably looked forward to it every week."

Then, referring to one of his own sons, Billy adds, "I'm going to get Willie one of those mugs."

Billy's father was instructed in turn by his own father, another accomplished storyteller. The stories, true ones, anchored Billy's mind back before the treaty, back before the Europeans, and his mind still inhabits those places. Through Billy Frank we can learn the whole progression, which casts many different rays of understanding on these times today.

And so, while Billy has been celebrated as a visionary, if we go deeper and truer we learn that he is best understood as a plainspoken bearer of traditions, a messenger, passing along messages from his father, from his grandfather, from those further back, from all Indian people, really. They are messages about ourselves, about the natural world, about societies past, about this society, and about societies to come. Some of the messages are simple and homespun: Teach your children to take pride in their workmanship when they put out their nets. Others are profound: You can't quell the fire of Indian sovereignty by arresting Indian fishermen. When examined rigorously — not out of any romanticism but only out of our own enlightened self-interest — these messages can be of great practical use to us in this and future years. Understood in this sense, there is no identifiable beginning or end to the story, but one place we might next visit is Billy Frank's true homeland at the time his father entered it.

In 1979, Willie Frank marked his 100th birthday and the fiftieth anniversary of his marriage to Angeline, shown here at age 88. Sixty years earlier, he secured his six-acre homesite under a Medicine Creek Treaty provision.

CHAPTER I

MUCK CREEK

Billy's dad was born in 1879. A half-century of non-Indian occupation had wrought many changes to the Nisqually village on the southern edge of the Muck Creek prairie. To enhance the fur trade, in 1833 the Hudson's Bay Company founded Fort Nisqually on Puget Sound near the mouth of the Nisqually River. The Methodists established a mission in 1839, followed promptly by the Catholics, who would be the most successful Christian proselytizers. Each year, a few farm families arrived on the Overland Trail or by ship. The small settlement of Tumwater started up in 1845.

By the early 1850s the policy of Manifest Destiny began to make its mark. An 1818 treaty between England and the United States had left the Pacific Northwest to the joint occupancy of the two nations, but an understanding evolved that the Americans would stay below the Columbia River. In 1846 the nations settled their claims, with the Americans taking control over what

Medicine Creek Treaty tribes reserved all lands on the reservation for fishing, and they also reserved fishing rights "at all usual and accustomed grounds and stations" outside their treaty land reservations. Fish weirs were common in larger upriver tributaries.

is now Washington and Oregon. As a result, the numbers of Americans in the southern Puget Sound area steadily increased. The town of Olympia, founded ten miles west of the Nisqually River, became a magnet for shipping and agriculture. The United States established Fort Steilacoom several miles north of the river. The Donation Land Act of 1850, the precursor of the general homestead policy, drew still more arrivals with its promise of free land in the Oregon Territory, which at that time included Washington. Although these developments assured good farmland and bustling communities to the Americans, they brought mostly woe to the Nisqually people.

As was true among all the tribes, European diseases cut a broad swath. Epidemics struck soon after the creation of Fort Nisqually. While wars and random violence would kill off some of the Nisqually, smallpox, measles, ague, and tuberculosis played far the greater role in the precipitous drop in Nisqually tribal population from about 2,000 in 1800 to fewer than 700 by the 1880s. And so, the deep changes worked by the new arrivals were both point-of-the-rifle and circuitous, at once engineered and random: "My dad always told me that the white man came over the mountain with a Bible in one hand

This Puyallup Indian weir is similar to a Muck Creek weir manned by the pre-statehood Nisqually to harvest precious salmon. Fish passage to spawning grounds was only partially restricted.

and a bottle of liquor in the other."

Federal officials and the churches, partners in assimilationist policy, joined in a determined effort to stamp out the Nisqually world view. "These people tried to teach us that our way of life was no good. Our way of talking was bad. Our way of thinking about life was bad. Our smokehouses were bad. Taking only what we needed was bad. Our offering back to the deer and the bear was bad. Our religion was bad." Their very names were bad. Billy's grandfather, Kluck-et-suh, shod horses for a farmer named Frank. The Indian agent, in the common administrative convenience of the time, renamed him "Frank's Indian." Billy's dad, Qui-Lash-Kut, became "William Frank."

The defining moments for the world Billy's dad was born into had come in the tumultuous mid-1850s, with the Nisqually–United States treaty and its aftermath. The treaties were a critical part of federal policy. Although the United States had obtained land title as against England and the European nations by means of international treaties, the tribes' land title remained in place. As Chief Justice John Marshall put it in the leading case, the tribes were "the rightful occupants of the soil, with a legal as well as just title to retain pos-

session of it." Only the United States could obtain the tribes' land title from them. This meant that homesteading could not legally proceed on Indian lands until the tribe transferred title to the United States. The treaties also had the advantage, from the United States' side, of confining Indian people to much smaller parcels of land. Creation of the reservations made the assimilation — that is, the eradication of Indian tribes as discrete societies and cultures — far more efficient.

Treaty time came for the Nisqually Tribe in late 1854. The driving force behind it was Isaac Stevens, President Pierce's appointment in 1853 as governor of the new and sprawling Territory of Washington, which stretched to northern Idaho and western Montana. Stevens also served as

Isaac Stevens (1818-1862), Washington Territory's first governor, concluded treaties with Northwest tribes in his role as Superintendent of Indian Affairs. The dictated terms of his first treaty (Medicine Creek, 1854) led to war within a year.

Superintendent of Indian Affairs. By 1854 Stevens, then thirty-six-years old, energetic and ambitious in the extreme, took on the task of negotiating treaties with the tribes of the whole territory. In less than a year he had negotiated eleven major treaties, most involving several tribes. From one standpoint his mission was a success, for after his non-stop caravan had done its work with the Flathead and Blackfeet tribes in Montana, Stevens had acquired most tribal lands in the Northwest in the name of the United States.

But his bullying tactics got him into trouble, causing resentment among the tribal peoples, which in several instances welled up into bloody rebellion. Stevens, who had graduated first in his class at West Point, saw treaty-making as a command-and-obey process, not a negotiation. He knew what he wanted going in and did not plan on departing from his course. The first of the Stevens treaties, at Medicine Creek with the Nisqually, Puyallup, and Squaxin Island tribes, was the start of it.

Stevens announced a treaty council for December 24, 1854, at Medicine Creek, a small stream the Nisqually called She-Na-Num, just to the west of the Nisqually River. The principal negotiators for the Nisqually would be Quiemuth and his brother, Leschi. Stevens had drawn up the treaty in advance.

The three tribes, while they never thought of land as a commodity that could be owned or sold, knew that Stevens' council would be a monumental event. George Gibbs, a member of Stevens' party, reported that the delegations of Indians, six to seven hundred in number, arrived over land and in cedar canoes and that they wore "all kinds of fantastic dresses." The talks took place out on marshy ground, the big firs and cedars on the sloping banks serving as backdrop. It rained most of the three days. The "treaty tree," a live fir then, a snag now, still stands as remembrance.

The Indian people, who spoke Salish, knew virtually no English. Stevens had an interpreter who was fluent in Salish, but the governor insisted that these discussions of transcendent matters be conducted in the 500 words of the Chinook jargon. Like pidgin English, the Chinook jargon was a rudimentary device for trade, a patchwork of English, French, and various tribal languages. How could it possibly speak to sovereignty, land ownership, fishing rights, assimilation, freedom, or the futures of societies?

Leschi (1808-1858), a Nisqually leader, had assisted a steady American move into the region after the British departure in 1846. But he would not assent to treaty terms taking away Nisqually villages and prairies. Military actions were taken against him. In 1858, he was unjustly hanged — until he was "*dead*, DEAD, DEAD."

In one sense, the inadequacy of the Chinook jargon mattered little. Stevens had his script and he meant to keep to it. The Nisqually leader Leschi — proud, fiery, and defiant — presented the main obstacle. He refused Stevens' request to draw a map of aboriginal Nisqually territory. He tore apart a document identifying him as a Nisqually subchief. He may have refused to sign the treaty altogether. Some witnesses said he did sign. Others said that the "X" beside his name was forged.

Leschi was incensed by the reservation assigned to the Nisqually. It was small — only two sections, just 1,280 acres or two square miles. And it lay up on the bluff to the west of the Nisqually River. The thickly wooded land gave no access to the river for fishing and took in none of the broad, sweeping prairies that characterized the watershed and that the Nisqually people loved. Squally means "prairie grass waving in the wind." The Tribe's name for itself, Squally-absch (changed to Nisqually by the whites), means "the people of the grass country."

But Stevens got his treaty signed, as originally written, by leaders of the three tribes. After the Senate confirmed it, the United States owned most of the southern Puget Sound and areas beyond — 2.5 million acres in all — free and clear.

Stevens included in Article Three a clause securing to the tribes the right to take fish "at all usual and accustomed grounds and stations, . . . in common with all citizens of the Territory." He knew the tribes would never sign without it. He also had his own reasons: fishing would feed the Indians, thereby reducing the federal government's responsibility for them; furthermore, during the presumably brief interlude that the tribes would continue to exist as discrete cultures, the incoming white farmers would want Indians available to harvest and trade salmon.

What Isaac Stevens could never have foreseen is that, more than a

"When the tide is out, the table is set." That was the stated belief of Nisqually Indians who harvested from bountiful tidelands and marine waters. In 1906, centenarian William Weahlup tends his shoreline salmon-smoking rack.

century later, courts would be confronted with vibrant Indian societies and his opaque phraseology about Indian fishing rights. Those judges would carefully note that Stevens had controlled the negotiations, had conducted them in the Chinook jargon rather than in tribal languages, and had written down the promises in English. The judges would further reason that, because the tribes had the right to fish before the Medicine Creek Treaty of 1854, and because the United States had a trustee's duty to protect the tribes, any relinquishment of their rights would require circumstances far more convincing of tribal intent than those orchestrated by Stevens.

The treaty definitely signaled an ending. It also marked a beginning. As Billy puts it, "They tried to move us off our river, off our plains. That's where our food was, our living was — all of our summer lodges, our winter lodges. Our salmon came back here. Basically, Leschi just said, 'We're not moving.' That's when the war started."

Leschi had a strong following among the Nisqually. He was a powerful orator with a commanding presence: he carried himself well — accounts typically emphasize his penetrating gaze. He was fair-minded:

the Nisqually looked to him to judge disputes among tribal members. And there was another reason why the Nisqually followed Leschi in rebelling against the events at Medicine Creek. He was rock-solid right about the treaty. Leave aside that it was a dictated set of words that rightly wounded the Nisqually pride. Beyond that, the treaty was wrong in substance, draconian in its implications. Forcing the Nisqually — a salmon and prairie people — onto two square miles atop a wooded bluff was mean-spirited, despicable. It was bad tribal policy, bad federal policy. What kind of leader, what kind of people, would let that stand?

The Nisqually clearly were digging in. Although Leschi had been well regarded by the settlers, rumblings among the white people began to target him as a troublemaker. Tensions moved to a new level after Stevens finished his treaty-making with the Yakama in June 1855. The Nisqually and the Yakama had close relations, and the horseback messages from one side of the Cascades to the other steeled the resolve of both tribes. The Indian agent to the Yakama was killed, presumably by tribal members. By late summer and early fall, Leschi was meeting with white people —

both territorial officials and settlers — trying to understand the full context and forestall violence. But Leschi was not going to let his people be moved to Stevens' reservation.

Like so many Indian wars, the Nisqually–United States firestorm was ignited by the confusions and miscalculations stemming from the gulf between such disparate cultures. On October 22, 1855, Acting Governor Charles Mason (Stevens was out in Montana negotiating the Blackfeet treaty) met with Leschi. Both men were firm in their positions. Mason was spurred on by a letter from James McAllister, a farmer since 1844 on the Nisqually Delta whose name would later be given to Medicine Creek, claiming that Leschi "has been doing all that he could possibly do to unite the Indians to raise against the whites in a hostile manner." Two days after his meeting with Leschi, Mason sent out nineteen members of Eaton's Rangers, a detachment of volunteers, to bring in Leschi and Quiemuth, probably reasoning that protective custody would work as a cooling-off period. The soldiers headed off toward the Cascade foothills to track down the two men.

The Nisqually immediately learned of this march on their leaders and saw it as an act of aggression. On October 27, the Rangers received word that McAllister and another volunteer, who had been sent ahead as scouts, had been shot and killed. This incident seems to have been based on a misunderstanding: the volunteers apparently wanted only to talk to the Nisqually but a tribal lookout interpreted their actions as threatening. Later that day, a group of Nisqually approached the soldiers' camp. Although the soldiers had orders not to fire first, Andrew Laws had trigger itch. He shot down one of the Nisqually men, and the war was on. As Cecilia Svinth Carpenter, Nisqually tribal historian, wrote, "Indian drums sounded throughout the foothills and not a canoe was seen in the river."

The conflict — pitched battles followed by interludes where the Nisqually, who knew the terrain better, hid out in the deep woods — went on for more than eight months. Leschi, who probably never had more than 300 troops, developed a disciplined military force. Billy's dad was born a generation after the war, but Billy's grandfather, while too young to fight, remembered the time well, and the memories have been passed down to Billy with precision.

From the elevated snow-packs of Mount Rainier to the salt waters of Puget Sound, a recurring dynamic prevails. Waterway flows into waterway in confluences from the Nisqually Glacier and highland Mashel River to the aquifer springs of Medicine Creek.

"Leschi trained his troops up on the Muck Creek prairie. My grandfather used to watch the soldiers disciplining their horses with a maneuver they called 'the wheel.'" The horsemen, about twenty in number, would line up in a straight row. Half of the horsemen — those on the right — would be facing north, the other half facing south. Then they would march their horses, always holding their line, like a long, single-bladed propeller. This training maneuver, of course, was never used in combat, but Leschi made regular and good use of it to create readiness.

Lives were lost on both sides during the many skirmishes. The greatest tragedy took place upriver, where Ohop Creek and the Mashel River join with the Nisqually River. Several families — people who were not warriors, people who wanted to stay away from the conflict — had retreated to the area, which was near Leschi's native village. Except for the few open prairies, it is steep, choppy country, the rugged foothills building up to Mount Rainer, thick with black-berry bushes and vine maple, good country to hide out in, but difficult to escape in if caught by surprise. In April 1856, Captain Hamilton J. C. Maxon and his troops came upon a small Nisqually encampment near Ohop Creek and killed everyone in it. Then Maxon and his men discovered a larger group of several families in a fishing camp near the confluence of the Mashel and the Nisqually rivers. Most of the people were women and children; a witness, Robert Thompson, counted only two men. Maxon ordered his soldiers to charge the defenseless Nisqually families. They slaughtered some seventeen Nisqually and wounded many more. Billy's dad heard many accounts of Maxon's Massacre and recounted them during a taped interview.

"Those Indians at the massacre, they were . . . up on the hill looking down at the place where the Mashel runs into the Nisqually. They said the soldiers came on them and the Indians all ran down the hill and swam across the [Nisqually] and ran up the other side. And the soldiers were shooting them from the top of the hill. There was a woman carrying a baby on her back and they shot her. She and the baby fell into the river and floated down. . . . Some of the young got away — climbed up the hill on the other side of the river. I don't know how many they killed, but there were a lot of them."

The territorial authorities finally took custody of Leschi in November 1856. His nephew Sluggia, who knew of Leschi's desire for peace, had been offered a reward for Leschi's capture. Taking his people's chief by surprise, Sluggia captured him and took him to Steilacoom, where Leschi was arrest-ed. Sluggia's breach of family and nationhood soon was avenged by Wa He Lut, one of Leschi's most able lieutenants. Wa He Lut killed Sluggia for his treason.

Three days after Leschi's arrest, the Territory tried him for the murder of Colonel A. Benton Moses, an American soldier. Leschi's lawyers argued — in addition to the fact that he had not committed the act — that this was done in war and should not be punished in civilian courts. The first trial resulted in a hung jury. After a re-trial of one day, a jury of local non-Indians found him guilty. On appeal, Leschi spoke to the Supreme Court of the Territory through an interpreter.

"I do not know anything about your laws. I have supposed that the killing of armed men in wartime was not murder; if it was, the soldiers who killed Indians are guilty of murder too. . . .

"I went to war because I believed that the Indian had been wronged by the white men, and I did everything in my power to beat the Boston soldiers, but, for lack of numbers, supplies and ammunition, I have failed.

"I deny that I had any part in the killing. . . . As God sees me, this is the truth."

Leschi's nobility carried through to the end. On February 19, 1858, three hundred people gathered around an outdoor gallows erected on a prairie near Fort Steilacoom and watched the condemned prisoner ride in on horseback. A few Nisqually stood at the edges of the crowd. The steady pounding of the old drums out in the distance, though, showed that all the people knew. The Nisqually leader's hangman, Charles Grainger, had his own vivid recollections.

"Leschi was a square-built man, and I should judge would weigh about 170 pounds. He was about five feet six inches tall. He had a very strong, square jaw and very piercing, dark brown eyes. He would look almost through you, a firm but not a savage look. His lower jaw and eyes denoted firmness of character. . . .

"He did not seem to be the least bit excited at all — nothing of the kind, and that is more than I could say for myself. In fact Leschi seemed to be the coolest of any on the scaffold. He was in good flesh and had a firm step and mounted the scaffold without assistance, and as well as I did myself. I felt then I was hanging an innocent man, and I believe it yet."

Some history blows away like ashes in the wind. Other history lives on as coals that smolder hot, that never go out. Once I asked Billy what he thinks of when he hears the phrase "the war." Billy answered without a pause: "The Leschi War." This is history that smolders on yet.

So by the time Billy's dad was born in 1879, the government-church-homesteader campaign had made its mark. Yet the traditional Nisqually ways remained strong. Their roots, after all, were sunk deep. Tribal accounts explain that the Nisqually originally resided far to the south, in Central America. As the glaciers receded, the people moved to the Great Basin, south and east of their present home. When the climate grew warmer and earthquakes shook the ground, the Nisqually crossed the southern slope of Mount Rainier and settled in the Nisqually watershed. Archaeologists have dated one Nisqually village at over 5,000 years old. Human occupation of the southern Puget Sound has been established at least 12,000 years ago, and those inhabitants are surely the ancestors of today's Nisqually Tribe.

It helped preserve the tribal ways, too, that the Nisqually lands lay at the far, thin edge of America's westward expansion. The white population of Pierce County in 1879 was 3,300. Tacoma had just 1,100 people. Olympia, the capital, remained a dirt-road village of perhaps 2,000 residents. Washington stood a decade away from statehood.

The traditions also lived on because of Leschi's legacy, which not only served to inspire later generations of Nisqually but also bore tangible results. Leschi's resistance was so fierce — and it so compellingly exposed Governor Stevens' over-reaching — that federal officials urged Stevens to meet again with representatives of the Medicine Creek tribes at the Fox Island internment camp in August 1856. Article Six of the treaty allowed for a replacement reservation and, in January 1857, President Pierce established one for the Nisqually.

The new reservation, while it totaled 4,700 acres (four times larger than Stevens' original creation), was still egregiously small. Still, it was a homeland in a way the first one could never have been. It straddled the Nisqually River. On the eastern side, it encompassed Nisqually Lake and part of the Muck Creek prairie, where Leschi had trained his men. Perhaps most important, it took in lower Muck Creek, where several of the largest of the thirteen tribal villages were located. This included the village in which Billy's grandfather lived. So, however painful the whole progression — reservation, war, and attempted assimilation — may have been, at least he never had to move his family.

One time I asked Billy if he could visualize what it was like back when his dad was young, and he told me that, yes, those times in the 1880s are vivid to him yet today.

"I can picture my dad riding on a horse with his dad. He'd be five or six years old, standing up on the horse's rump, holding on to his dad's

20 Muck Creek

The Nisqually Indians built their streamside villages along the region's major upland prairies. Fires were used to burn back encroaching timberlands and to maintain cultivation grounds for staple foods — edible bulbs, berries, and roots — and medicines. Prairies also provided pasture for Nisqually horses.

shoulders. They'd be riding across the Muck Creek prairie. The grass would be blowing. I know what it was like, because my dad did it with me when I was a little boy and he told me that his dad had done it with him."

Billy also has clear pictures in his mind, both from what his dad told him and from his own explorations, of life down on the river in the late nineteenth century. The salmon still ran strong and the Nisqually, unlike most tribes confined to small reservations, needed no government rations. Nisqually families consumed an average of 500 salmon each year.

"When I was young, there were still cedar buildings there, down by the river. There were pieces of timber, different things, lying around.

"I can picture Dad. Maybe he'd take fifty salmon. Then he'd go over to a gravel bar, lay the fish down, and butcher them right there. His dad and granddad taught him. I knew how this worked because he taught me everything he and his granddad did, and my kids do it today.

"Then you take the fillets and weave three cedar sticks through them crossways. The stick up near the gills comes out on both sides so you can hang the fish on poles in the smokehouse. But you don't hang them up the first day. They'd drop off the sticks. So you let them drip and dry out a little, overnight. Then Dad would get his fire going in the smokehouse the next morning. He'd hang the fish on poles across the eaves of the smokehouse. The smoke comes out of the cracks in the smokehouse.

"How long he'd leave them in would depend on what he wanted. You can smoke them just a little bit and get what white people call kippered. Or you can leave them in long to cook more, smoke more. You can get jerky if you want, hard as a rock, and they'll never spoil or rot or mold. Later, you put them in water to soften.

"Down by the river with the smokehouse was the ceremonial house. The medicine people would use that and you didn't go in there. They had sweat houses by the river, too."

The Nisqually also kept their distinctive canoes — handsome and utilitarian — down by the river. "Those things took a couple of years to make. I know, because my dad showed me how and I've made them. You have to go to the logjams in the spring and find the right tree, one of the small cedars that washed down the river. Then you've got to let it sit and dry in the shade, not in the sun. Then you do all the cutting and hollowing and carving.

Ferryman Sam Piyelo, in 1905, poles his flat, shovel-nosed cedar canoe in the Nisqually River adjoining Muck Creek prairie. Nearby is Willie Frank's 1884 reservation family allotment and home village.

"The residential area was on the prairie, up above the river. My dad lived in a cedar home. They took a big tree struck by lightning. The grain was straight as can be. They'd use a stone wedge and a mallet to make a crack. Then they'd split it into a perfect plank, thirty, forty, fifty feet long. You didn't even have a knot in those old-growth trees.

"We had everything back when Dad was a boy. The hunters would come back with furs and skins and meat. The Sound was close, only eight miles downriver. Dad would take a canoe down to the mud flats at low tide for the clams, the oysters, the geoducks. He'd always say, 'When the tide goes out, our table is set.'"

Muck Creek prairie was a source of both food and majesty. "They knew how to burn the prairies without burning the woods. Today they call it controlled burns. It was magic.

They'd burn it so the potatoes and onions and carrots would come up the next spring. That beautiful prairie. And our mountain is sticking up off by the side."

The Nisqually went up the watershed to the flanks of Mount Rainier in the fall. The huckleberries were the main objective, but exploration and discovery were part of it, too. "Dad used to go up to our mountain every fall. The mountain was alive. There were hot spots on the mountain. Dad wasn't a scientist. He didn't know about thermal things. He didn't use that kind of language.

"But they visited the thermal springs and they actually walked inside the glacier. Big holes. They wanted to know what was in there. Big chunks of ice. Inside the mountain. That's where the river starts, a special place. He talked about it; his dad talked about it."

With all its diversity, life revolved around the salmon. Muck Creek was home to one of the Northwest's great chum salmon runs. "Most of the rivers don't have any runs in December, January, and February. But Muck Creek had a large spring up above Dad's village. This spring will pop up, maybe around Christmas, maybe the first week in January. *Boom*, all this water comes out and

starts flowing to the river. The chum salmon are waiting for it and will head straight toward Muck Creek and that spring."

Billy often recounts that his dad, telling of the Nisqually watershed of his youth, always called it "paradise." I gained some small understanding of this on an early-autumn daybreak hike on the six-mile trail that encircles the Nisqually Delta. Today it is a national wildlife refuge. I have rarely been surrounded by such a profusion of natural plenty. Nearly a dozen flocks of Canada geese came honking in. I passed at least twenty blue heron and many more mallards. Blackberries, salmon berries, and blueberries ripened. Two harriers perched on snags, watching for voles. A clutch of harbor seals worked the lower mile of the river, knowing that the fall chinook were coming in. The mist lifted with the incoming sun and, as Billy puts it, "Now our mountain is sticking up over there." I had the Delta all to myself.

I began thinking about Billy's dad's words. Yes: paradise. But as I hiked on the edge of the broad, low-tide, thick-smelling mud flats, it became ever clearer to me what he meant. For Americans today, when the word is used outside of a religious context, "paradise" means a strikingly beauti-

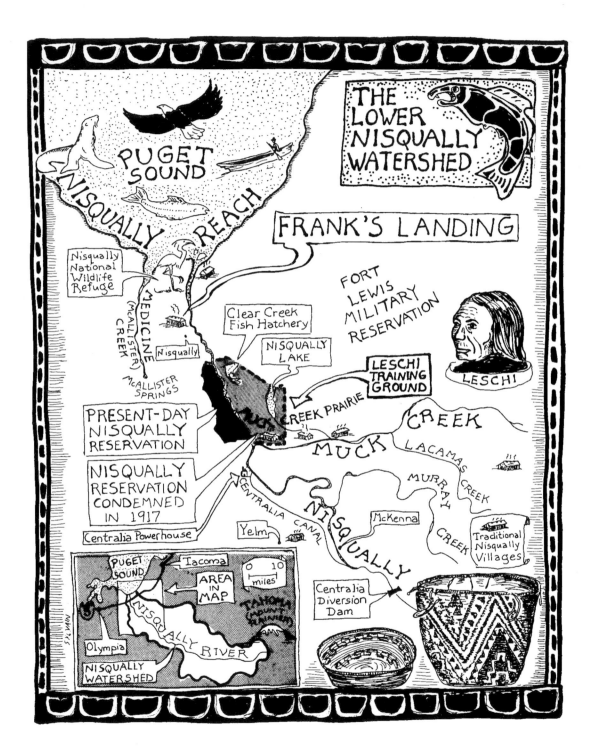

THE LOWER NISQUALLY WATERSHED

PUGET SOUND

NISQUALLY REACH

FRANK'S LANDING

Nisqually National Wildlife Refuge

MEDICINE (McALLISTER) CREEK

McALLISTER SPRINGS

Nisqually

Clear Creek Fish Hatchery

NISQUALLY LAKE

FORT LEWIS MILITARY RESERVATION

LESCHI TRAINING GROUND

LESCHI

PRESENT-DAY NISQUALLY RESERVATION

CREEK PRAIRIE

MUCK CREEK

LACAMAS CREEK

MURRAY CREEK

NISQUALLY RESERVATION CONDEMNED IN 1917

Centralia Powerhouse

CENTRALIA CANAL

NISQUALLY

Yelm

McKenna

Traditional Nisqually Villages

Centralia Diversion Dam

PUGET SOUND

Tacoma

AREA IN MAP

0   10
miles

TAHOMA MOUNT RAINIER

SYLVAN

Olympia

NISQUALLY RIVER

NISQUALLY WATERSHED

ful place, a place that endures in our memory. But we leave paradise — we leave many paradises. Later that morning, I would be off to my duties.

For Billy's dad, paradise — from this delta up the river and its valley and its prairies to the mountain where the river is born — was a homeland so generous that it gave you everything you and your family could possibly need. It filled a person completely up. And you were part of it, not separate. You were umbilically connected to paradise. Just one paradise. You didn't go off to other duties. You couldn't. You were connected.

You learn a lot about this from Billy's dad's first experience with the white man's school. The Indian agents pressured all the parents to send their kids off to federal boarding school. When Billy's dad was six, his father reluctantly took him some forty miles on horseback, out of the Nisqually watershed, up past Tacoma, to the boarding school in Federal Way. Two weeks later, the father, upon going back up to the school to visit, was told: "Your son's not here." It turned out that the boy had just left with George LaPlate, a schoolmate from Chehalis. Billy's dad made it all the way back home on foot. It took him two days.

Willie Frank, at a 1910 hop picking encampment, stands behind his aunt, niece, and sister. Hop picking fostered spirited intertribal bone-gambling and joyful family reunions.

"Now you tell me," Billy says. "Did that little guy know this country? Hell, he'd been all over this country. They didn't go toward Canada. They knew where they were all the time. He got home to Muck Creek and his friend kept going to Chehalis. He always taught me: You never get lost. Always follow the water. The water will get bigger. Creek, stream, river, sound, ocean."

Billy's dad returned to grade school for a few years, but his life was back home. "Dad had a wagon and a horse on Muck Creek. If you had a wagon and a horse, you were rich. You could go up to Taholah and haul the fish to market in Aberdeen and Moclips, Grays Harbor. He had everything.

"One time a guy asked my dad what his Social Security number was. That didn't make any sense to my dad: he said, 'Why would I need some number?' Then the guy asked how he made a living. My dad said, 'I don't need to make a living. I just fish.'"

In 1931 Billy's dad and his mom, Angeline, had their only child, William Frank, Jr. — Billy Frank. Although his mother and father could never have imagined the life that Billy would lead, they could tell early on

that this boy — smart, athletic, outgoing, and energetic, as well as a considerable hell-raiser — had a spark in him. Billy grew up around Nisqually speakers, but he learned the majority language as well, and one guesses that his favorite parts of it come in the shade of blue — his discourse liberally dusted as it is with "hells," "Jesus's," and "goddammits" — organic parts of his spirited and easygoing way of communicating. Billy went through ninth grade, but his real education was with the salmon people and the river, always the river.

But he did not grow up in the village on the edge of Muck Creek prairie.

By 1916, as the pressures built toward World War I, the United States rapidly increased its military readiness. Army posts were plums and Tacoma wanted one. Farm, forest, and prairie land in the lower Nisqually valley would make a perfect site. This included Muck Creek prairie and the Indian lands down by the river. The base would be 60,000 acres or more, of which Indian lands were but a small part. In that sense, Tacoma and the United States Army were not targeting the Nisqually Reservation. But they failed to heed the special character of the Indian lands. The lands had been promised by a treaty. They were held in trust by the United States of America.

Pierce County filed the condemnation proceedings and then transferred the lands to the army as part of Fort Lewis. This was proper for the private lands but was flatly illegal for the Nisqually Reservation. Federal agencies, much less counties, have no right to condemn Indian trust lands unless Congress expressly authorizes it, which Congress had not done.

Illegal though the Pierce County condemnation was, the military did not even wait for its conclusion. As one account explains: "In the winter of 1917, the United States Army moved in trespass upon the lands of the Nisqually. Indian families were summarily ordered to leave their homes and not return until advised of permission to do so. Some families were loaded up on wagons and transported to other parts of the Nisqually River valley and left to find shelter among trees or makeshift protections against the weather."

Congress called for an investigation, which was completed in 1920. The Secretary of the Interior wrote: "I am still of the opinion that it would be unwise to obtain these lands by condemnation . . . and evict the Indians therefrom, who would no doubt object strongly to removing from their homes." The Secretaries of War and the Interior both emphasized the patriotism of the Nisqually: "[We] feel very strongly . . . that the splendid spirit manifested by the Indians in promptly surrendering their old homes, of inestimable value to them, to aid our country should not go unnoticed. . . ." But the Nisqually of the 1910s, dispirited, disorganized, and dispossessed, had no way to fight back as they had done in the 1850s, and as they would do again in the 1960s and beyond. The land was never restored. Congress ratified the condemnation and set up a small fund for replacement land. Fort Lewis now had two-thirds of the reservation.

This removal from their homes, in the dead of winter, shattered the lives of the Nisqually. Many fled the area to the homes of relatives at Puyallup, Chehalis, or Quinault. Some suffered pneumonia. Josephine Pope, the wife of Billy's dad, died within a year. Later, in 1928, he married Angeline.

"All of a sudden they said to my dad, 'You don't have a place to live anymore.' That, and losing his wife, must have been a blow to the young man that he was. But he wasn't going to give up. He was a steady, quiet guy.

He didn't look for trouble. I tell Willie this. You go around trouble. Go around it.

"So he walked around looking for land. He lived in a tent down by the mouth of the river for a couple of years. Finally, in 1919, he decided on six acres along the river. It was owned by a farmer, Wint Bennett, and he sold it to my dad. That place became known as Frank's Landing.

"How do you have the patience to deal with these people? You've been crapped on time and time again, how do you do it? His patience was in his bringing up, in the carving of the canoes, living near that river with all that water going by him, the salmon coming back every year, coming back every year."

CHAPTER 2

NISQUALLY RIVER

"That river was my life. You understand it right from when you were a little boy. The winter floods, the spring floods, the low summer water. We lived right on the bank, right near the edge of tidewater. At Frank's Landing you know exactly when the tide comes in and when it goes out.

"And there was a relationship between your life as a little boy and the salmon. You knew that every year the salmon came back. Spring salmon, summer salmon, fall salmon, then the winter run of chum salmon up to Muck Creek. Then the cycle would start over again.

"We lived in that river all summer. Every day, fishing, swimming. We had an old wooden bridge. The Old Road, we called it. It's not there anymore — it got torn down after World War II. But back then, we'd dive off it. We had a swing attached to it. We'd get up on the bank, get on that rope and swing way out into the deep water, then let go, swim back, and do it again. We'd drink the water.

"Frank's Landing was a meeting place for all the children, not just the Indian kids but all the farmers' kids too. All the Braget kids would come over. We were neighbors.

"We saw the changes in the river every year. The river would meander and we used to run up to the new logjams it made. We were always looking for cedar logs to make canoes. We'd climb all over the logjams and dive off. We'd walk six miles or more up the river to find those logjams. On the way we'd stop at the farmers' orchards and eat apples."

As a boy, Billy loved going down to Nisqually Reach, where the river hits Puget Sound. The family would make day trips in the canoes, down with the tide, back up to Frank's Landing with the tide. The Reach was on a main flyway. "When I was a kid, we had huge numbers of birds. Eagles. Ducks. Geese. Big white swans. God, those white swans were beautiful birds." On the day trips, the Franks would bring back oysters, clams, and fish. "Jesus, there were flounders all over the place. We'd just wade in, wiggle our feet and, when you felt one, just reach down and grab it. We'd keep the ones we wanted and throw the others back."

But new pressures were building. In 1935, when Billy was just four, his dad suffered his first arrest for illegal fishing. More and more non-Indians were moving into the Puget Sound area, and the state began singling out Indian fishermen who were not getting state licenses or following state seasons or take-limits. The Nisqually River spring run of chinook — the biggest and best-tasting fish — went into decline in the late 1940s, falling victim to the unregulated offshore commercial boats and to hydroelectric development.

The end of World War II proved to be a decisive moment for the Pacific Northwest. The Boeing Company, whose sales had skyrocketed during the war effort, became the anchor of Puget Sound's economy, continuing to produce military aircraft during the Cold War and expanding to include commercial planes by the 1950s. Electronics and aerospace industries moved in, and international trade flourished. The suburbs mushroomed in response to people's appreciation for the region's clean air and outdoor lifestyle. In eastern Washington, a burgeoning demand plus good growing conditions in the Yakima and Wenatchee valleys and elsewhere led to irrigated bumper crops of apples, pears, and other specialty fruits and vegetables. Washington as a state grew from 2.3 million people at the close of World War II to nearly 6 million at the end of the century. The Puget Sound area expanded three-fold, shooting from 1 million in 1945 to 3.3 million in the late 1990s.

The non-Indian salmon take rose sharply in the years after the war. Forty-six Puget Sound commercial gillnetters fished for sockeye in 1945; the number leaped to 322 in 1953, to 637 in 1957; there were 121 seiners in 1945, 452 in 1961. Salmon and the aerobatic steelhead were pursued avidly for recreation by newcomers flooding into the Northwest. Washington put a daily two-fish limit on sport fishing for salmon, but an annual commercial license, with no daily limit, cost $15. As a result, sport fishermen regularly purported to take up commercial fishing.

Population pressures brought wholesale habitat destruction. The short, steep rivers running from the Cascades to Puget Sound created outstanding opportunities for generating electricity to fuel industrial and residential development; the City of Tacoma seized one of these opportunities with its generating facilities on the upper Nisqually River. The hydroelectric projects of Tacoma and the City of Centralia, to which we will return, pounded the salmon runs on the Nisqually.

At the same time, fueled by the baby boom, the housing industry cranked up and the nation looked to the Northwest for timber. The Forest Service enthusiastically responded. By 1965 timber harvests on the national forests climbed to a level eleven times higher than before the war and, in the process, trashed valuable salmon habitat. Private timber companies worked their lands ever more intensively. Urban and suburban development, including road and highway building, ate away at the vitality of the watersheds. Poisons — especially 2-4-D and other pesticides used in forestry and agriculture — found their way into the rivers. "When I was a kid," Billy laments, "the fish were so damn clean and healthy."

The quick flashes of silver that embody the natural bounty of the Pacific Northwest went into free fall. The 1960 non-Indian commercial chinook take dropped by more than half from the 1940s. Other species went into similar declines, or worse.

All the troubles — of race, of the environment — that had been lying dormant but dangerous for decades welled up after World War II and threatened to rework once again the lives of the Nisqually people. By the 1960s the state's sporadic arrests, like Billy's first one back in 1945, had escalated into a relentless law enforcement campaign of raids and stings.

As Judge George Boldt would find in 1974, after exhaustive hearings, Indian fishermen had not wasted fish or harmed the runs. Regardless, for the state enforcement officers a decade earlier, it was a holy crusade and they would give no quarter. They saw these Indians as renegades who were flouting state conservation laws, sensible and valuable laws that had been adopted for good reasons. They saw this lawless Indian conduct as a main reason the runs had crashed. Now the salmon runs themselves hung in the balance.

Billy Frank's early life gave no particular indication of the role he would play in the historic confrontations over the Pacific salmon. At six, he started out as a first grader at the Nisqually Grade School. The two-room wooden building was close enough to Frank's Landing that he could walk to school. He spent his last two years of elementary school at the Lacey Grade School and then moved on to junior high in Olympia. His formal education ended after the ninth grade.

© Mary Randlett

But if it is true that Billy's first three decades scarcely suggested what was to come, it is also true that a standard account of a budding activist's education and jobs rarely reveals the personal qualities, churning and building over the years of a young life, that will cause a person to assume the burden of challenging accepted authority on behalf of a sacred cause. Rage — rage at history, rage at the present — will show up on no résumé. Neither will the growing realization that Leschi's spirit lives on in your own soul.

The old Nisqually Grade School was four blocks distant from young Billy Frank's home. A similar trek took him to "Nisqually" for mail and groceries. The wee wayside town and general delivery post office vanished with the construction of Interstate-5 in 1968.

Billy fished from his canoe and peddled the salmon, suffering a few random arrests and confiscations. He also took on odd jobs out of the American Federation of Labor Union Hall in Olympia. The union members had first call on the jobs, but Billy, who had no union card, was a good worker and regularly scared up construction work on the roads and sewer systems. In 1952, at the age of twenty-one, he fulfilled his dream of becoming a U.S. Marine. "I took real pride in that, the discipline, the hard training. I was in good physical condition, always have been." After two years with the Corps, he returned to Frank's Landing, his salmon trade, and construction work.

"Al Bridges and I were out on the river in the fall of 1964. It was an afternoon like this one, sunny, warm." Billy was talking from the stern of his eighteen-foot aluminum boat. He turned off the motor so we could drift while he showed me this stretch of river, about a mile from the mouth of the Nisqually.

"Al and I were in a canoe that Johnny Bobb had made for me. I always kind of smile when I think of Johnny. I'd be out walking around and I'd see all these ladders — just two by fours — nailed to trees. They were all over the place. One time I saw Johnny hammering one of them

Billy Frank, U.S. Marine (1952)

Al Bridges (1922-1982) and his wife, Maiselle, raised their three daughters, Suzette, Valerie, and Alison, at Frank's Landing. When game wardens rammed and capsized Billy's now-famous canoe, Al was arrested too.

and I asked him what he was doing. He told me that he couldn't see so good any more and that he staggered when he walked and that the deer always heard him coming. He was a subsistence hunter and he wasn't getting any deer. 'So,' he tells me, 'I put these ladders up in trees next to deer trails, get up in the tree, and when a deer comes by, I shoot him.'

"Johnny Bobb. What a guy. He's having trouble getting deer and what does he do? He puts these goddam ladders up in the trees.

"And he knew how to carve a great cedar canoe.

"Anyway, I was taking Bridges out to get his nets. We were just having a good time. We were right about here and — see that slough over there?" Billy pointed toward the east side of the river.

"I shouted out, 'Bridges, Jesus Christ, there's the state!'

"At the beginning, these guys had no idea how to run a boat on this river. They didn't understand the river. We figured out their favorite hiding places. If there weren't any ducks around, we figured the state guys were in there and had scared away all the ducks. But they got real serious about this. And this was the time of Selma; there was a lot of unrest in the nation. Congress had

funded some big law-enforcement programs and they got all kinds of training and riot gear — shields, helmets, everything. And they got fancy new boats.

"So all of a sudden this boat was coming at me and Bridges like a bat out of hell. We turned upstream and tried to run them into another net but we never made it. Those bastards rammed us at full speed and knocked us clean over. We had our hip boots on and it was harder'n hell to swim. I honestly thought I was going to drown.

"We finally got to shore and other guys were waiting for us. 'Stop or we'll shoot.' These guys had a budget. This was a war. Indians never did trust any of these guys and don't to this day. We didn't write those laws. That's why we try to write the laws today.

"They hauled us by boat up to a marina in Tacoma. We were still soaking wet. By the time we got released, it must have been midnight. We got fined and had our salmon and nets confiscated. They confiscated Johnny Bobb's canoe, too.

"That was one of the worst of all the episodes, but stuff like that was going on all the time. It was nearly a daily event to get hassled by those guys. It was a good day if you didn't get arrested. After a while, I didn't even bother to tell people at the Landing because they already knew: 'If we don't come back home, call C. J. Johnson.' He was the bail bondsman."

By the mid-1960s Frank's Landing, along with the demonstrations led by Bob Satiacum, Ramona Bennett, and other Puyallups on the Puyallup River in Tacoma, had become the focal point for the tribal assertion of treaty rights in the Northwest. The Landing also lay at the moral center of the tribal sovereignty movement nationally, as tribes began to climb up out of the termination abyss of the 1950s. The goal of termination, which Congress had announced as the official Indian policy, was to end, forever, the special status of Indian tribes. Sell off the reservations. End the longstanding education and health programs. Make Indians subject to state laws. Assimilate them into mainstream American society. This policy was every bit as focused and dangerous as the attacks on land and culture during Leschi's day.

The drama at Frank's Landing began in earnest in January 1962, when the state mounted a major raid on Nisqually fishermen during the winter run of chum salmon bound for Muck Creek. The state's campaign did not subside for more than a decade. The confrontations flared up, of course, only when the salmon ran. It is worth noting that, in between runs, life was generally peaceful at the Frank family compound on the broad flat at a bend of the river, along the west bank. Four modest frame houses sat amid the old maples, fir, cedar, and dogwood. Billy's mom and dad lived in the family house, closest to the river. Billy's sister, Maiselle, had married Billy's fishing partner, Al Bridges, of both Nisqually and Puyallup blood, tall, trim, and elegant in his red headband. They had three daughters: Alison, Valerie, and Suzette. Billy and his wife, Norma, lived in another house with their son, Tobin (called "Sugar"), and their daughter, Maureen. The other home was for Billy's nephew, Herman. Billy's dad kept a garden — corn, rhubarb, and squash. Maiselle grew flowers.

The families struggled to patch together a living. The salmon, when the state didn't confiscate them, gave some subsistence and a small income. During the summers, Al, Maiselle, and the girls worked nearby farm fields. Billy went on the road as a lineman, erecting tall towers and

At age thirteen, during the October 1965 confrontation with fisheries wardens, Alison Bridges Gottfriedson became a veteran of the Fish War skirmishes. Years later, as a skilled fisherman, she expertly motors the swift, turbid Nisqually River.

Maureen Frank (1958–1977) lifts high a salmon from her father Billy's catch, just days after his jail release in 1968. Two years later, her younger brother, Tobin ("Sugar"), at age nine, would experience his first arrest.

Treaty rights claims centered on a Puyallup River reservation fishing encampment in 1970. A 300-man police force surrounded the encampment, indiscriminately firing tear gas and shotguns and arresting all 62 occupants.

In 1968, gillnet inefficiency was demonstrated amidst hundreds of visible king salmon in Olympia's Budd Inlet waters. No salmon were caught, but observer Billy Frank was carried off to jail.

canoe or skiff unloading salmon from a gillnet. Usually the Nisqually would give passive resistance — dead weight — and five officers or more would drag the men up the rugged banks toward the waiting vehicles. The dragging often got rough, with much pushing and shoving, many arms twisted way up the back, and numerous cold-cock punches. The billy clubs made their thuds. Sometimes the Indian men struck back. Sometimes Indian people on the banks threw stones and sticks at the intruders. The stench of tear gas hung in the air.

The Nisqually women got involved too. Film footage shows Maiselle Bridges and Billy's wife, Norma, clinging desperately to the nets as the officers dragged them forcefully up the rocky river bank. As with all the blood struggles of minority people for freedom the world over, a sorrow, a poignancy shared the air with the tear gas. Yes, all the young, clean-cut, crew-cut officers charged down the banks toward their duty, fixed on fulfilling their oaths to enforce the law — good law, so they believed. And yes, for some of them, their eyes remained cold during the ensuing brawls. But in other young eyes, one could see the questioning, the sadness. Why does it have to be this way? Is this right?

stringing electrical lines in British Columbia, Montana, Idaho, Washington, and down to Oregon.

But during the runs, Frank's Landing was hyperactive, white hot. The surveillance was continuous. There were scores of raids, many of them — preserved both in front-page photographs and a great amount of film footage — ugly, heartrending brawls. In time, the banks of the Nisqually merged with the schoolhouse steps of Little Rock, the bridge at Selma, and the back of the bus in Montgomery.

The game wardens — a dozen to more than fifty — would descend the banks in a stone-faced scramble toward a few Nisqually men in a

Federal court decisions barely fazed state fisheries agencies. Their continued enforcement actions were quickly challenged by Indian fishermen. Norma Frank is shown here under state arrest being dragged from her boat on the Nisqually River (1969).

The people at Frank's Landing learned to endure the grimness of the arrests, combat, confiscations, fines, and jail time. They had a banner to carry. It had fallen to their generation to defend the treaty and Leschi's legacy. Though the odds might have seemed long to others, their spirits were high. They knew that Billy's dad and a few other Nisqually fishermen had obtained a federal court injunction against state interference with their fishing, back in 1937. They had no truck with the Washington state courts, but they had faith that the federal judiciary would honor the treaties. They used the term "supreme law of the land," and they understood what it meant.

They had support. Frank's Landing hit the news and gradually came to be recognized in the active 1960s as a place to go and honor a noble cause. Actor Marlon Brando came, lending his name to the effort. Canadian Native folk singer Buffy Saint Marie sang to her sisters and brothers. Luminaries of the future — Richard White, later a leading historian of the American West, and Elizabeth Furse, who became an Oregon congresswoman in the 1990s — stood on the banks of the Nisqually and heard the messages. The black comedian Dick Gregory drew national attention and

also lightened the skies. The Indian people liked him and his humor. At one press conference, a reporter asked Gregory if he had been offered tribal membership. His response was, "No thanks, I've got enough problems."

Business also was part of the scene. One point, after all, of the Medicine Creek Treaty was the commercial sale of fish. The tribes had always traded salmon with inland tribes for goods from their regions. After white people came, as Isaac Stevens knew, Indians sold fish to the farmers. In modern

© Mary Randlett

Within tidal reach, sloping banks and gravel bars made Frank's Landing a natural boat launch and mooring site. It once featured the lower Nisqually's last fixed-cable ferry crossing. Willie Frank's original 1884 allotment was the farthest upriver on the Nisqually reservation. Frank's Landing is the Indian land farthest downstream.

At a long-used butchering table, Michael Hunt and Joe Carson clean fresh silver salmon for shipment to New York and to volunteer sellers in California's Golden Gate State Park (1970).

times, the salmon made up one part of the struggle to break the grip of poverty.

So, when the Nisqually could get their fish out of the river and past the police, one objective was to get some of the salmon to market. Local buyers would pay only 10¢ a pound, but a pound of salmon would fetch a dollar in more distant markets. Some of the most delicious moments at Frank's Landing during the 1960s and early 1970s took place after nightfall, as Indian people loaded bright, freshly cleaned Nisqually salmon into a plain, white truck bound for Union Square in San Francisco, properly launched into the dark with a Frank's Landing send-off of muffled laughter and sotto voce whispers of "Go get 'em!" and "You're doing the Great Spirit's work!"

It was kaleidoscopic. Family. Armed arrests. Fierce resistance. Indian people from all over. Celebrities. Black Panthers, SDSers and hippies. Common well-wishers. Constant surveillance from across the river. Smoke emerging from the smokehouses and wood stoves. Commerce and the processing of fish. Indian humor and laughter. Earnest talk of treaties, federal courts, and the Constitution.

Yet, in certain ways it was an organized chaos. Billy's dad finally had stopped fishing in the early 1960s, in his eighties, but he was an anchor, giving people encouragement, walking around and tapping the maples and cottonwoods with his cane to show the old trees he was still there. Billy was an anchor too, but his life was down on the river — his river, the river that ran in his blood — defending that river and his people and their way of life. His defiant image and words went out over the newsreels and in the papers and were passed along by word of mouth, giving inspiration to Indian people and displaying to the larger world the fury and staying power that Native people would summon forth in defense of their land. "We aren't," Billy would proclaim time and time again, "going anywhere."

While Billy at that time was not

© Mary Randlett

For generations of tribal fishermen and distant canneries, Frank's Landing was the principal Nisqually buying station. Buyers brought their customary portable scales to temporary stations after the last fish house disappeared.

a tactician ("I was not a policy guy. I was a getting-arrested guy."), his sister, Maiselle Bridges, was a major strategist in getting out the Frank's Landing story and organizing the drive to secure the treaty rights. Her three daughters also took part. Alison and Suzette took on all manner of

organizational tasks. Valerie proved to be a riveting speaker: "We set the net and waited for the state. We have to let them know we're not going to stop fishing. We have this treaty right, the supreme law of the land under their Constitution. It's a treaty we're fighting for."

Hank Adams speaks at a 1970 press conference at the Seattle Center of the American Indian Women's Service League. With Adams are Alison Gottfriedson, holding one-year-old Powhattan Mills, and Mike McCloud.

At the very center of the strategy was the activist Hank Adams — tireless, fiery, chain-smoking, lights-out brilliant, and soul-deep loyal to a sacred undertaking. Adams, an Assiniboine and Sioux from the Fort Peck Reservation in Montana and a great-grandson of Sioux Chief Yellow Eagle, came to Washington as a child during World War II. From day one, he was a gifted student. But it figured that no college could hold his restlessness and his 6:00 a.m. till noon sleeping hours — and, after two years, the

University of Washington proved in 1963 that it could not. Adams had more pressing business. Although still in his teens, he had steeped himself in Indian history and law, including the extreme assimilationist policies that Congress and the Bureau of Indian Affairs pursued during the 1950s and early 1960s. Indians had long been mostly passive on the national scene, leaving a leadership vacuum. Along with other young, charismatic Indian intellectuals — notably Vine Deloria, Jr., Clyde Warrior, and Mel Thom — Hank Adams quickly became a national leader, bent on change. He joined the National Indian Youth Council as an organizer and in that capacity arrived at Frank's Landing in February 1964.

Adams dove into his new task, mapping out a grand scheme but also precisely crossing every *t* and dotting every *i*. "You're too patient," a Nisqually friend told him. "No," Adams responded, "I'm most impatient. I want to take the time to do it right so I won't have to spend my life here." But for once Hank Adams had it wrong. He never left, and Frank's Landing is still his life.

Adams' first job back in 1964 was to organize the wildly successful demonstration — 2,000 supporters showed up — at the state capitol in

Don Matheson addresses a rally of treaty rights supporters at Washington's Temple of Justice, at which plaintiffs for the *United States v. Oregon (Sohappy)* litigation, from Cooks Landing on the Columbia River, also spoke (1968).

Olympia. He enticed Charles Kuralt to bring out his CBS show to cover the saga at Frank's Landing. He brought in Brando. He instigated and facilitated three stirring film documentaries: *In the Shadow of the Eagle; Treaties Made, Treaties Broken*; and, especially, Carol Burns' *As Long as the Rivers Run*. He helped to conceive and to secure the funding for publication of

Uncommon Controversy, a report sponsored by the American Friends Service Committee on the Washington fishing rights controversy. *Uncommon Controversy* — a well-written, fair-minded, scholarly treatment of the issue — went into several printings.

The grass-roots organizing, the political rallies, the documentaries, and *Uncommon Controversy* may begin to suggest the range and depth of Hank Adams' vision. There is much more.

"I came back to my office," University of Washington law professor Ralph Johnson recalled, "one day in the spring of 1966, after teaching my class in property law. There were at least fifteen Natives in my office. I could barely get in the door. Hank Adams and Bob Satiacum were the leaders.

"They told me that they wanted me to teach a course in Indian law to undergraduates. I resisted at first. I had no background at all in the field."

Ralph Johnson was in good company. At the time, other than a course in Oklahoma on Indian land titles, no one in the country was teaching Indian law. But few people have had much luck resisting Hank Adams. Over the next two years, Johnson taught the undergraduate course, and

in 1969 he began teaching Indian law in the law school. Johnson continued until his retirement in 1999, having taught American Indian law longer than anyone in history. And, although trained as a traditional legal scholar, he didn't mince his words about the fishing issue. "This was an injustice. It was entirely wrong. The state was being repressive, racist."

By the late 1960s, a great many things had been set in motion. Perhaps most important, the cause of the Nisqually and other Northwest tribes had acquired a dignity, a moral content that was understood and appreciated by a great many Americans. This was of no small moment. In a democracy, where tiny minorities by definition lack the numbers to influence policy by their votes, recognition of their rights often in fact turns upon morality and the appreciation of it by a wider citizenry that does have the numbers. Sometimes that morality is manifested in legislation, as it was with the sweeping civil rights laws of this same era. In the case of the Nisqually, where the morality was already embodied in a federal law — the 1854 treaty — the logical recourse was to enforce it in the federal courts. They knew they would be walking a long road.

CHAPTER 3

GEORGE HUGO BOLDT

After six fishermen were jailed for contempt, a resistance organization was formed in 1964. Canoeing on the Nisqually, SAIA founders Janet McCloud (bow), Don Matheson, and Al Bridges (navigator) prepare to lead a Frank's Landing "fish-in" (1966).

The Indian fishing rights dispute flared brightest along the Nisqually and Puyallup rivers, but the controversy also affected the Stevens treaty tribes across Washington and Oregon, Idaho and Montana. Similar controversies had erupted in northern California and the Great Lakes states. For the tribes, enforcing the treaties meant establishing three fundamental points: tribal fishers could fish free of state regulation; tribes, as sovereign governments, had primary regulatory authority on the reservations and at off-reservation sites; and the tribes had the right to harvest a substantial part of the runs. This third asserted treaty right — to a specified allocation of fish — was especially contentious because it would require the state fisheries agencies to set more restrictive fishing seasons and bag limits on non-Indian trollers and gillnetters so that the requisite amount of fish could be taken by the treaty fishermen. The complicated and emotionally charged legal issues, their sprawling geographic reach, and the plethora of tribes and of state and federal agencies made it nearly impossible to control the situation in a strategic sense. But the tribes were quickly moving out of their passive mode of the 1950s and early 1960s into a much more assertive posture. They were determined to try. And no one was better at trying than Hank Adams, who by then was firmly ensconced at Frank's Landing.

An opportunity to get into federal court presented itself on the Columbia River. In 1968, Yakama fishermen Richard Sohappy (a much-decorated army veteran) and his nephew, David, were arrested for fishing with gillnets, and they wanted to bring a test case. Adams obtained a small grant from the NAACP to support the litigation. Professor Ralph Johnson and others filed *Sohappy v. Smith* in the United States District Court in Portland on behalf of the Sohappys and twelve other Yakama tribal members. The defendant was an Oregon fish commissioner.

The case was assigned to Judge Robert C. Belloni. Federal officials, moved by the repeated state criminal prosecutions of treaty fishermen, were persuaded to weigh in on behalf of the Sohappys, and the resulting case, *United States v. Oregon*, was consolidated with *Sohappy v. Smith*. The issues went to trial in

49

1969, and Judge Belloni ruled for the tribes. The treaties were valid. The tribes had special, federally guaranteed rights, outside of state law. Judge Belloni also ruled that the tribes had the right to an allocation of fish. He articulated the tribal allocation as a "fair share" of the harvestable salmon (all parties agreed that only the "harvestable" portion of a run would be allocated to Indian and non-Indian fishers, so as to allow for sufficient escapement to ensure perpetuation of the runs). The 1969 *Sohappy* ruling was a major breakthrough.

But, while the idea of a "fair share" was enormously helpful to the tribes, the Oregon decision did not define the percentage of fish to which the tribes were entitled. Could a tribe take, say, 5 percent of the harvestable fish in a particular run? A third?

Half? More? What was a "fair share"? Eventually a court would have to decide.

After the *Sohappy* decision, the United States remained committed to a strong tribal position. In 1970 the United States filed *United States v. Washington*, on behalf of the tribes in the Puget Sound and Olympic Peninsula areas that had been parties to the Stevens treaties. The calculus in the State of Washington had changed. Now the federal government had thrown its prestige behind the Nisqually and the other tribes. The Justice and Interior Departments would provide excellent lawyers, especially George Dysart, who for years had dedicated himself to the Indians' cause. Equally as important, the United States would fund the expert historians, anthropologists,

and biologists who would be needed to research, and to testify on, the circumstances surrounding the Stevens treaties.

In the meantime, Hank Adams and Tulalip leader Janet McCloud had requested assistance from the Native American Rights Fund (NARF), the new national Indian law firm. The tribes would benefit from having their own lawyers in addition to the federal attorneys who were litigating the case for the United States, as trustee for the tribes. David Getches, executive director of NARF, became the lead counsel for many of the tribes. The legal services programs that helped bring justice to Indian country beginning in the 1960s also played a key role: John Sennhauser, Michael Taylor, and David Allen of Seattle (later Evergreen) Legal Services served as co-counsel to Getches. Alvin Ziontz, more senior, with the stature of a leading member of the Seattle bar, represented the Makah, Lummi, and Quileute tribes. Several other lawyers, including Alan Stay, who would represent the Nisqually after the trial, participated for the tribes in the complex litigation.

United States v. Washington was assigned to Judge George H. Boldt, a tough law-and-order jurist. An army veteran, Boldt had tried several high-

profile cases, handing out stiff sentences to Teamster leader Dave Beck and underworld boxing figure Frankie Carbo. Known both for his fairness and his strict insistence on courtroom decorum, he declared a mistrial for the Vietnam protestors, the Seattle Seven, but then held them in contempt for their outbursts during trial and sentenced them to six months. A slight, gray-haired man who wore a bow tie, Boldt had no background in Indian law, but this case would prove to be the most significant in his distinguished twenty-six-year tenure on the federal bench.

The tribal lawyers in *United States v. Washington* were clear about arguing against any state regulatory authority (and in favor of broad tribal authority) over treaty fishing. They agonized, however, over how to handle the issue of a percentage allocation, for which there was no direct legal precedent.

The tribal position, as it evolved, did not explicitly call for a percentage split. The tribes relied on the rule of treaty interpretation that the treaty words must be read as the tribal negotiators would have understood them. The report prepared for the tribes by Dr. Barbara Lane, an anthropologist, showed that Isaac Stevens had been expansive in assuring the

To frustrate a 1966 "fish-in," State Fisheries wardens swept the Nisqually to remove all surface nets. In answer, Billy Frank poled to his submerged "sinker" net, which yielded four steelhead to (r. to l.) Herman John, Roy Kalama, Al Bridges, and Leonard Squally.

Indians that, while their land holdings would be reduced, the treaty would not restrict their fishing. (As one example, at the Point No Point treaty negotiations, Stevens told the tribes that "This paper secures your fish.") The tribal representatives at the treaty negotiations, in other words, thought that the treaties would allow non-Indians to move into the area and share in the fishing, but without interfering with the age-old tribal practices. Thus, the tribes contended that the treaties reserved to the tribes "sufficient fish to meet their needs" — and that this actual-needs standard was not limited to 50 percent or any other fixed formula.

The lawyers for the tribes did, however, introduce the 50 percent notion in a limited context. Looking to definitions from 1828 and 1862 dictionaries, Getches found authority for the proposition that "common" (the critical phrase in the Stevens treaties was "in common with the citizens of the Territory") meant "equal." Therefore, the argument went, while the judge should focus primarily on what the Indians understood, the dictionary definition suggested that even the non-Indian negotiators could not have seen the treaty as giving up more than half of the tribes' right to fish. The tribal

attorneys knew that an equal division would vastly improve the situation of the tribes, but they feared that throwing any percentage on the table might cause Judge Boldt, very much an unknown quantity at the time, to settle on some lesser amount. The state, remember, was arguing that the tribes had no special rights at all. Basically, the tribal attorneys floated the 50-50 split but did not press it.

The idea of a generous allocation — as high as 50 percent or even more — was generally supported by two leading U.S. Supreme Court decisions. *United States v. Winans*, in 1905, affirmed the right of Yakama Indians, members of a Stevens treaty tribe, to fish at traditional stations on the Columbia, even though the area had been homesteaded to a non-Indian. The Court upheld the off-reservation rights, writing that any doubtful treaty phrases should be construed as the Indians themselves would have understood them. The Court explained its reasons for protecting Indian fishing rights, which the tribes possessed before the treaties, in memorable language: the right to fish was "not much less necessary to the existence of the Indians than the atmosphere they breathed." In 1942, the Court in *Tulee v. Washington* gave another protective reading to the treaties, holding that Washington could not require off-reservation Indian fishermen to obtain state licenses.

The attorneys for the United States needed some persuasion. When *United States v. Washington* was initially filed, their position was that it would be sufficient to reaffirm the "fair share" notion in Judge Belloni's *Sohappy* decision. But after the selection of a special trial counsel, Stuart Pierson of Washington, D.C., they took a stronger stance, agreeing with the tribal lawyers that the "fair share" formulation had been a necessary stepping stone, but that they should now ask Judge Boldt to set a more precisely articulated — and high — measure of allocation for the tribal treaty rights. The federal lawyers did not, however, decide upon a specific formula at that time.

The ambivalence of the federal and tribal attorneys over the exact strategy continued to show as the case unfolded. Working closely together, they took the unusual step of filing a joint Post-Trial Brief, signed by Getches on behalf of "All Plaintiffs' Attorneys." The brief did not rely on the 50-50 allocation, asserting instead that the right was not limited by the 50 percent benchmark but rather guaranteed sufficient fish to meet tribal needs. At final oral argument, however, they took slightly different tacks. Pierson, for the United States, recommended a 50-50 allocation. Ziontz and Getches, for the tribes, argued that there should be no numerical tribal quota, and that Indian fishers should be entitled to take as many fish as were necessary to meet tribal needs.

When *United States v. Washington* was filed, the State of Washington reaffirmed its longtime stand that Indian treaty fishers were like any other citizens and were fully subject to state regulation. Some Washington state court cases suggested that result. In 1916, the state supreme court had written this in *State v. Towessnute*: "The premise of Indian sovereignty we reject. . . . The Indian was a child, and a dangerous child, of nature, to be both protected and restrained. . . . Neither Rome nor sagacious Britain ever dealt more liberally with their subject races than we with these savage tribes, whom it was generally tempting and always easy to destroy and whom we have so often permitted to squander vast areas of fertile land before our eyes."

Ah, history. Who was the better historian, this Washington Supreme Court judge or Leschi's hangman? But that kind of judicial declaration was red meat in the 1960s and 1970s for Washington officials caught up in their war on the tribes. Jack Metcalf, then a state senator and later a congressman, said: "You can't have superior rights; you can't have a hereditary aristocracy . . . that has more rights than other people. That won't work in this country." Walter Neubrecht, head of the Washington Department of Game, bluntly asserted the states' rights view: "We had to bring in our full force and arrest anyone who had resisted or was interfering with us in the performance of our duties."

Powerful forces in state government, then, insisted on going to the mat. No special treaty rights. This is purely an enforcement matter. Just read the state laws.

More troubling as a legal matter was the so-called *Puyallup I* decision in 1968. That opinion, written by Justice William O. Douglas, had found that the state could regulate off-reservation fishing if "reasonable and necessary" to achieve "conservation" of the species. This seemed to give support to an argument the state had made all along — that it was regulating Indians to protect the species. As the tribes saw it, the state was singling out tribes and discriminating against them so that non-Indians could take the fish; the state's crackdowns had nothing to do with true

conservation. In 1972 Ralph Johnson authored a seminal article in the *Washington Law Review* sharply criticizing *Puyallup I*. He wrote that the state scheme was not aimed at conserving the salmon but rather was an allocation among user groups, including Indians. The allocation to Indian tribes, he argued, had already been done in the treaties, and the treaties were supreme over state law.

In 1973, while the *United States v. Washington* litigation was moving toward trial, the U.S. Supreme Court handed down the case referred to as *Puyallup II*. The issue was whether Washington could ban all net fishing for steelhead. Justice Douglas' opinion, following Johnson's reasoning, found that the state's system was not "necessary for conservation." Instead, it was intended to allocate steelhead to hook-and-line sport fishermen and wrongly attempted to rule out Indian net fishers. Indians had always used nets, and the state could not prohibit Indian net fishing under these circumstances.

And so in *Puyallup II* the Supreme Court had rejected the state's sweeping conservation argument. William Rodgers, tribal lawyer and law professor, had briefed the case well. Professor Johnson's article was razor sharp and just. Justice Douglas had

himself grown up in the Yakima valley and was believed to have some sympaties for Indians. But could it also have mattered that, after *Puyallup I* and before *Puyallup II*, one Hank Adams had befriended one Cathy Douglas, the wife of the Justice? And that Cathy Douglas, herself a lawyer, had visited Frank's Landing and had, like many before her, become imbued with the rightness of the tribes' position?

Before the Boldt trial, the Washington Department of Fisheries, which had jurisdiction over all salmonids except steelhead, unleashed a thunderbolt. The agency announced that it would support the idea that "fair share" meant a full one-third to the tribes, with one-third to non-Indian

sport fishers and one-third to non-Indian commercial fishers. Yes, the morality was settling in. The fisheries department could see that the tribes had a compelling case. But the unbending Department of Game, with jurisdiction over steelhead, held firm. It always did, whether on the banks of the rivers or at the bar of the Court. No special treaty rights.

The month-long trial was held in the fall of 1973, in the federal courthouse in Tacoma. Dr. Barbara Lane and biologist Jim Heckman gave expert testimony for the United States and the tribes. The Indian presence was palpable in the old, wood-paneled courtroom, which now held all the hopes and dreams of the fishing tribes of the Pacific Northwest, all their histories and futures. Many Indian people sat silently in the gallery. Several testified. Billy recounted the many arrests and gear confiscations. Tribal elders, including Lena Hillaire of Puyallup, eighty-six years old, and Billy's dad, ninety-five at the time, told their stories, including the history that had been handed down to them. Judge Boldt, always attentive in court, was especially so during the elders' testimony. He leaned forward across the bench, rapt.

On February 12, 1974, Judge Boldt issued one of the most sweeping and significant judicial rulings in the history of the Pacific Northwest. The "Boldt decision" (as with the "Belloni decision" in Oregon four years earlier, the ruling quickly became personalized) came down for the tribes on substantially all counts, including the 50-50 allocation. The 203-page opinion was rich with history, as it should have been: after all, the Supreme Court had said in *Winans*, back at the turn of the century, that treaties should be construed as the Indians themselves would have understood them. If Leschi, a fair man, a judge for his own people, could have read with his piercing eyes this luminous chapter in the history of American justice, he would have nodded in approval.

In the last analysis, the critical provision in the Boldt decision — the 50-50 division of the salmon and steelhead between Indian and non-Indian fishers — must be attributed to the incisive mind of Judge Boldt himself. From the tribal perspective, it was logical and just, even conservative. For thousands of years, before the treaties were signed, the tribes had organized their lives around the salmon. They had no limits on the number of fish they could take. At treaty time, they insisted on protecting their right to fish, and Stevens assured them they could. But from the stand-

point of non-Indian fishers in the late twentieth century, the 50-50 idea was radical, a travesty. Indians made up less than one percent of the population. When the trial began, they were taking (due, it is true, to rigorous state regulation) about 5 percent of the total salmon harvest. The tribal and federal attorneys had made the case for a large allocation to the Indian fishermen and had tentatively suggested an equal split, but in the end it was Judge Boldt's sense of history, law, and fairness, and his courage, upon which this great decision rested.

Judge Boldt's resolve was severely tested for years after his historic 1974 ruling. His order — more so than nearly any court decree ever handed down — was extraordinarily difficult to enforce. The ruling encompassed twenty-one tribes, several hundred tribal fishers, thousands of non-Indian commercial fishers, hundreds of thousands of sport fishers, and dozens of rivers, each with several fish runs annually.

Beyond that, the physical circumstances were in constant flux. Take, as a hypothetical example, the fall chinook run in the Puyallup River in 1977. Assume that a harvestable run of 8,000 fish had returned to the river the year before. But this is September 15, 1977, and the tribes, supported by

Father and son here walk along the sacred river that runs through their family's land. In 1982, Willie Frank was a witness in his last legal case to protect the Nisqually. "I guess we're the oldest things around," he would say after he reached age 100. "Me, the mountain up there, and the river, yeah." For him, "to launch my last canoe without regret" was an Indian prayer fully answered.

their biologists, are asking for an off-shore closure, while the state and the non-Indian commercial trollers, backed by their biologists, assure the court that no off-shore closure is needed. The fish will reach the trollers' coastal fishing grounds before entering the river, where the Indians fish. Judge Boldt will have to decide how many fish the trollers will be allowed to harvest so that the Indian fishers on the river can take their 50 percent share. One key question is the size of the run: in 1977, how many chinook are heading down from the Gulf of Alaska toward the Puyallup River — 8,000? 2,000? 20,000? Inconveniently, the answer is swimming in the ocean with the chinook themselves, who are still a couple of hundred miles north of Puget Sound, and the Puyallup River salmon are mixed with thousands of fish headed for other rivers.

Judge Boldt appointed a Court Advisor, initially the respected University of Washington biologist Richard Whitney, to advise the court on scientific matters and resolve disputes where possible. On disputed matters, the Court Advisor would receive information from one person from the state and one from the tribes; he would then make a recommendation, which was almost always upheld, to Judge Boldt. The arrangement worked quite well and avoided many contested court proceedings. Nonetheless, for the scientists — and for the judge, when they could not agree — making such estimates (and many other kinds of difficult factual determinations), often on incomplete data, was challenging at best, a nightmare at worst. And the hypothetical 1977 example cited above represents just one run on one river in one year.

These logistics were compounded by the recalcitrance of the state and the non-Indian fishers. One might expect the matter to have been resolved soon after Boldt's 1974 ruling: the Ninth Circuit Court of Appeals affirmed the Boldt decision in 1975, writing a comprehensive opinion, and in 1976 the United States Supreme Court declined to take the case, making Boldt's ruling final. The Boldt decision was now the "supreme law of the land," meaning that under the Constitution it overrode state law.

But Washington officials and their commercial and sport constituents continually fought the ruling. As Judge Boldt issued closures for non-treaty fishing (the changes were sufficiently numerous as to require a toll-free "hotline" for fishers), it was incumbent on the state to carry them out. The Department of Fisheries, however, regularly refused to enforce Boldt's orders. Non-Indian fishers held "fish-ins" in defiance. On those relatively few occasions when the department did seek enforcement, state court judges — effectively partners with the state administrators — usually threw out the charges. This led to literally hundreds of contested enforcement orders from Judge Boldt. (West Publishing Company, which prints federal and state court opinions, took the rare step of publishing a "Compilation of Major Post-Trial Orders," thirty-seven in all, longer in total wording than the original Boldt decision.) These outlaw fisheries became the norm — along with hangings of Judge Boldt in effigy and a proliferation of bumper stickers: "Slice Belloni, Screw Boldt"; "Can Judge Boldt, Not Salmon"; "Let's Give 50 Percent of the Indians to Judge Boldt." Boldt held firm, but, as Fay Cohen has explained in *Treaties on Trial*, the non-Indians' far-flung

Indian rights were attacked by organized non-Indian groups during *United States v. Washington* (1970-1998). They defied the 1974 Boldt decision on the waters, in state courts, through ballot initiatives, and with many protest rallies.

vigilantism took its toll: "Massive illegal fishing continued for years following the decision. The numbers indicate the magnitude of the problem: when the court ordered closure of the fishery in the fall of 1976, fisheries patrol officers saw some 247 fishermen fishing illegally. In 1977, according to evidence later introduced in court, an illegal harvest of 7,036 chinook, weighing 109,204 pounds, was caught in Bellingham Bay alone, while 33,359 chum, weighing 337,623 pounds, were caught illegally in northern Hood Canal."

The depth of the state's resistance was underscored by a remarkable observation made by the United States Supreme Court. In 1979, responding to the state's persistence in trying to overturn the Boldt decision, which by all legal lights was final, the Court agreed to hear a related case that called the original ruling into question. In reaffirming substantially all aspects of the Boldt decision, the Supreme Court, quoting from the court of appeals decision below, made this direct comparison between minority rights in Puget Sound and the Deep the tribes, for example, were notably unhappy when he was assigned to the case, concerned that Boldt would be blind to the long tribal experience and the unique body of law that had grown up out of it. In its own way, the answer is disarmingly simple, but at the same time it speaks volumes about America's judicial system when it works at its best.

When we think of the high moments of our jurisprudence, we instinctively turn to people such as John Marshall and Oliver Wendell Holmes, judges who came to the bench with strong convictions and who carried them out. George Boldt, however, brought no preconceptions to this case and proceeded in much the same methodi-

Judge George H. Boldt, after years of enforcing his 1974 decision, visited Indian reservations and tribal fisheries to witness the results of his decrees. Tribal officials Dorian Sanchez (l.), George Kalama (r.), and Billy Frank welcome Judge Boldt among the Nisqually.

South: "The State's extraordinary machinations in resisting the [1974] decree have forced the district court to take over a large share of the management of the State's fishery in order to enforce its decrees. Except for some desegregation cases, the district court has faced the most concerted official and private efforts to frustrate a decree of a federal court witnessed in this century."

Why did George Boldt, a conservative, an Eisenhower appointee, a tough, no-nonsense judge with no previous knowledge of Indian law, come down this way? The lawyers for

Removing the hanged effigies of Judge Boldt from the premises of federal courthouses became a mundane duty of the U.S. Marshals. More dangerous work was the halting of non-Indian harvesters who defiantly took the tribes' shares of salmon fisheries.

cal fashion as did Frank Johnson, a fellow district court judge who was courageously hard at work on the Alabama desegregation cases, 2,500 miles to the southeast.

Boldt explained that he spent "days and days on end" reading "all the great decisions on Indians and fishing rights. Over and over again, all the great minds who dealt with the problem of Indians put in their opinions that we were taking away from the Indians their rightful heritage. . . . Historically, the Indians would never sign a treaty unless they'd retained their prerogatives to fish in their usual and accustomed places." Boldt did acknowledge that his 50-50 split was not somehow set in stone, and that the allocation issue called for him to exercise his judgment: "Somebody else might have ruled that the Indians were entitled to just a third or a fourth of the catch."

Professor Ralph Johnson gives this explanation: "During a long, long period of preparation for this trial, he educated himself and came to what he believed was the truth. He was strong-minded enough that he would apply simple justice." Speaking to Boldt's post-trial orders, Professor William Rodgers reflected that "he was open minded, and when he made it up he was a giant. A lot of judges waver but he never did."

Billy Frank has his own observations about Judge Boldt: "That judge listened to all of us. He let us tell our stories, right there in federal court. He made a decision, he interpreted the treaty, and he gave us a tool to help save the salmon.

"That judge went through a lot. I knew him personally, his wife and his family. That judge was . . . I don't know the word. . . . His own society didn't want to have anything to do with him, the clubs, the golfing places. The bumper stickers said, 'Can Judge Boldt.' They ridiculed him.

"But he made a decision and it's intact today. He gave us the opportunity to make our own regulations, our own management systems. We have to think about what he did for us; that's a responsibility we have. We can't ever forget that responsibility."

It is not something he talks about much, but Billy meant what he said about responsibility. The man who came over the mountain never got to Billy with the Bible he held in the one hand, but he did get to him with the bottle he held in the other.

Billy had made history on the river. He, along with Al Bridges, symbolized the Northwest Indian fisherman, embattled but tenacious, ever determined to vindicate his people and the treaty. But off the river he was sometimes unreliable. He missed some meetings. There were times when all the justified anger would erupt and unleash itself — so different from his control today, so at odds with what his father had taught him.

"In the Marine Corps, I never drank. But by the 1970s, I'm a tired guy. I'd been dragged up a lot of rocks by a lot of policemen. Then I'd sit in jail for two, three, four days. Then I'd get out and go on a march for the treaties, or whatever. Today, you don't see so much drinking among Indian leaders, but back then you did. There was a lot to celebrate, a lot of excitement.

"Then you're a lineman, on the road for a month or two, maybe more, at a time. All the linemen drank. One

Valerie Bridges (1950–1970), a valiant fighter, was a strong link among all families at Frank's Landing. She was their true unifying force in the darkest hours. Valerie's last court trial, in April 1970, was reminiscent of Leschi's last trial in 1857.

day I had a hangover and I didn't want to go to work. I just said to myself, 'This crap interferes with what I have to do, with how I perform.'"

There were other factors. Valerie Bridges, Maiselle's daughter, Billy's niece, looked up to him. Tough, direct, articulate, and caught up in a sacred cause, Valerie pleaded with him to quit. "Uncle," she would say, "you've got to *stop*. Uncle, you can change the world if you would just *stop*."

Then, in 1970 at the age of twenty, Valerie Bridges drowned at Frank's Landing. She was swimming after a long day's work in the field on a hot summer's day. There was no hint

of foul play. Perhaps she developed muscle cramps.

Valerie's words never died. Maiselle Bridges and Hank Adams continued the discussion on her behalf. Billy knew they were right.

Judge Boldt's decision also played into it. The opinion had not just reaffirmed the treaties and allocated 50 percent of the fish. It had also recognized the tribes' sovereignty and ruled that tribal governments had the authority to regulate their members — and the responsibility to do it right. All the Indian leaders knew that the state would be looking over their shoulders.

Valerie Bridges (1969)

Billy Frank met Sue Crystal when she was assigned to acquire lands for Wa He Lut Indian School's permanent site. Since the birth of their son in April 1982, Sue has continued as an attorney in high state government offices, while Billy has retained chairmanship of the Northwest Indian Fisheries Commission.

In 1974, shortly after the Boldt decision, Billy enrolled in an intensive recovery program at the Shickshadel Institute near Sea-Tac and he hasn't taken a drink since. The decision was a turning point in his life. In 1977, he lost his daughter, Maureen, and his granddaughter, Cabaqhud, to a car wreck. Hank Adams worried that the tragedy might send him back to drinking, but it never did.

About that time, Billy met lawyer Sue Crystal, protégée of Professor Ralph Johnson and special assistant to Senator Warren Magnuson. Billy and Norma had separated, but they kept in close touch until Norma's death in 1987. As one person told me, "He had to take care of Norma. He didn't want to cause her any trouble. He feels good about it. So does Sue."

Billy, Sue, and their son Willie, born in 1982, have a tightly knit home life. "Being with Billy," says Sue, "is like floating on a steady, easy river. Billy's life is turbulent, but Billy is not. He's the happiest person I know. He's completely at peace with himself. The river will flow to the sea. Period."

And the age-old teaching continues on. "Billy is teaching Willie to be a man, an Indian man in this world. He just quietly tells him things: how to treat people, how to treat the earth,

how to treat women." Sue pauses. "The last part is my favorite part."

Billy Frank, Jr., had played a critical role in one turbulent era. Now he was ready to train all of his many talents and energies on a very different kind of challenge.

Billy saw the possibilities the moment the Boldt decision came down. "We won a lot in that decision, but we also had a lot of new things to do. Plenty of federal funding for tribal fisheries management came in right away. 'Hey,' we realized. 'We can hire technical people. We can do it right.' God, those were exciting times. There was so much we could do."

© Mary Randlett

Three Nisqually generations at Frank's Landing in 1982: Qui-Lash-Kut (Willie Frank, Sr.), age 103; Kluck-et-suh (Billy Frank, Jr.), age 51; and Qui-Lash-Kut (Willie Frank), 6 months. Named for his grandfather, Billy will pass his name to his firstborn grandson in the Qui-Lash-Kut and Kluck-et-suh lineage.

Guy McMinds, from Quinault, and Dutch Kinley, up at Lummi, had founded an intertribal fish commission for Washington tribes. Maybe this promising group could bring Indian values and expert management to the rivers. The Nisqually and the other watersheds had been wrecked. What good would the treaty rights be if the runs continued to go down?

The Indians knew these watersheds better than anyone. Maybe, now that Judge Boldt had confirmed the tribal rights, the counterproductive conflict could end. Maybe the Indian rights could be a galvanizing force against bad development. Maybe the tribes could take their rightful place at the center of the effort to save the salmon.

Heady thoughts. But these were idealistic times in Indian country. Down on the river Billy had always been patient and he'd never quit, just like his dad had taught him. Maybe now he could begin to apply some of those ideas about how to treat the rivers and the land, ideas that had been passed down to him by his dad and many before him.

CHAPTER 4

FORT LEWIS

Billy Frank is known today as an architect of consensus solutions, a leader whose vision and personal skills have brought cooperation to previously contentious interest groups. And it is true that most consensus efforts to protect the lands and waters of Washington, and many of the efforts in the Pacific Northwest, bear Billy's fingerprints. Yet there is reason to pause here. The image of a group endeavor to heal wounds to the natural world and at the same time meet the economic needs of the human community carries a softness, an aura of form without substance. The term "collaborative effort" can rightly raise suspicions of fluffy, unenforceable promises. Has the lamb lain down with the lion?

Good and lasting cooperative agreements, however, need not have any of this. A movement to achieve progress on a complex public issue may end in the handshakes and hugs of a consensus resolution duly reached, but it must begin with a precise formulation of goals by the have-not interest group. Then, in between the goals and the handshakes, lies the toughest stretch — years, sometimes decades, of patient, persistent work in the form of analysis and development and execution of tactics. There must be a clear-eyed understanding of the enlightened self-interest of all the players, big and little. There is much jockeying for position. A recalcitrant bureaucrat may need a wake-up phone call from a superior or a member of Congress. The status quo may need to be jarred by a carefully timed press conference or well-placed op-ed piece. And the haves who refuse to budge — by dint of power, or intransigence, or both — may need to feel the sting of a lawsuit.

Billy became a master of the long stretch of time, the time of hard work and hardball tactics, that must precede the smiles. If it is true, as I think it is, that Billy moved to new terrain after the Boldt decision in 1974, it is equally true that he never abandoned the warrior mentality he had honed on the banks of Frank's Landing during the Fish Wars. Big heart, yes; collaborative processes, yes; widest smile in the State of Washington, yes — but what mattered in the long term were the fish and the river and the land and the people. They must be honored and protected before there would be any hugs or handshakes.

After signing a Secretarial Order to protect Indian rights under Endangered Species Act measures, Commerce Secretary William Daley (l.) and Interior Secretary Bruce Babbitt stand with Billy Frank and Quinault leader Joe DeLaCruz (r.) in the White House Treaty Room (June 5, 1997).

There is no better way to perceive this strategic determination than in the effort, over the course of more than two decades, that Billy has put forth in order to restore the river that gives life to him and his people, that gave life to those who went before, and that must continue to give life to those ahead.

In the mid-1970s, the Nisqually Tribe began the kind of revival that was taking place on Indian reservations across the country, especially in the Pacific Northwest where the Boldt decision clarified tribal rights, generated new federal financial support, and lifted spirits. In 1974, the Tribe adopted a fishing ordinance to implement the tribal regulatory power recognized by Judge Boldt. The Tribe then formed a fish commission, hired a biologist, and set up a tribal court. In 1975 and 1976, under Zelma McCloud as tribal chair, the tribal council addressed the matter of physical facilities for this rapidly growing government. For years, the council had variously met at the Boy Scout cabin in Yelm, the Assembly of God church on the reservation, and the old schoolhouse Billy had attended as a boy. Tribal headquarters, such as they were, had been located in a back room of the Methodist church in Yelm and in a rented house on the lower Nisqually River. McCloud and other leaders obtained a federal grant for a new tribal center — a fine facility, still in use today — to house the tribal operations.

In March 1977, Billy Frank sent a seventeen-page memorandum to Nisqually tribal members which would prove to be a defining moment for the Nisqually watershed. As the Tribe's newly appointed fisheries manager, he wanted to lay out an ambitious program to restore the

Tribe's fisheries and gain approval to implement it. The memorandum went out at the historic low point for the tribal fishery. The runs were way down. Judge Boldt's decision of three years past had yet to be fully implemented.

Tribal members knew all too well of the steady decline in the salmon and steelhead take. As early as 1910, the City of Tacoma had put in the La Grande hydroelectric project, with a dam located forty-four miles above the mouth of the river, to meet some of Tacoma's needs for electricity. Far more serious was another dam, constructed by the City of Centralia in 1929 at river mile twenty-six. Centralia took 320 cubic feet per second — a relatively small amount during the winter but three-quarters of the river, or more, during the summer and early fall — and diverted it out of the river into a canal. The Centralia Canal ran for eight miles to a cliff above the river, where the diverted water was sent plunging down a penstock, through the turbines of a powerhouse, and back into the river. Like Tacoma's dam, Centralia's six-foot-high diversion dam had no fish ladders and no screens at the head of the canal; with no screens, juvenile salmon were swept into the canal and killed in the turbines.

The development boom that took off in the mid-1940s made matters much worse for the Nisqually fishery. In 1944, Tacoma vastly expanded its operations in the upper watershed. It replaced its existing dam with a two-dam complex, including the 285-foot-high Alder Dam, which flooded seven miles of river and canyons with Alder Reservoir. In 1955, Centralia doubled its water right to 720 cubic feet per second, now taking at least half the river during most of the year and nearly drying it up during many of the summer dog days.

Water law not only allowed but encouraged the two growing cities, Tacoma from the north and Centralia from the south, to reach out of their own watersheds and rework the Nisqually River. Under the first-in-time/first-in-right doctrine of western water law, the cities had to pay nothing for the water itself. Nor was there any regulation of their operations. So the law gave carte blanche to the developers but had no safeguards for the salmon, the Nisqually, the other citizens of the watershed, or the river itself.

The city water projects hammered the salmon. In the case of Tacoma's dams, it is unclear whether they actually blocked any fish runs. Natural waterfalls in the narrow canyon

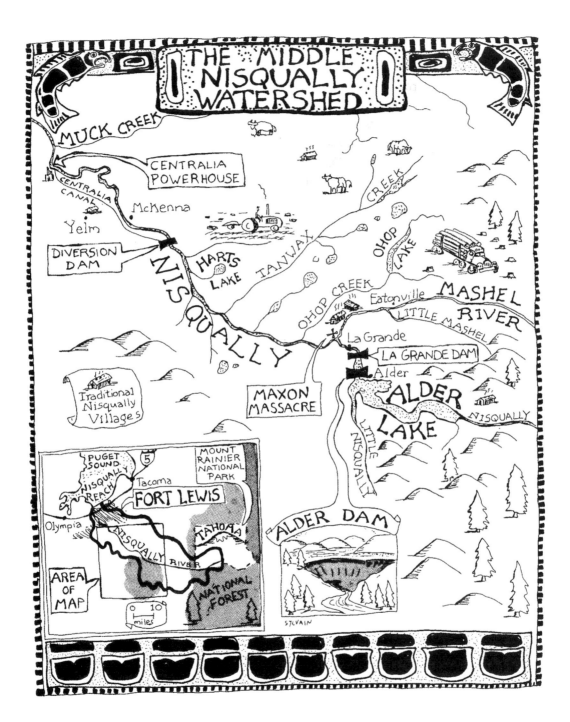

THE MIDDLE NISQUALLY WATERSHED

MUCK CREEK

CENTRALIA POWERHOUSE

CENTRALIA CANAL

McKenna

Yelm

DIVERSION DAM

NISQUALLY

HARTS LAKE

TANWAX

___ CREEK

OHOP LAKE

OHOP CREEK

Eatonville

MASHEL RIVER

LITTLE MASHEL

La Grande

LA GRANDE DAM

Alder

Traditional Nisqually Villages

MAXON MASSACRE

ALDER LAKE

NISQUALLY

LITTLE NISQUALLY

PUGET SOUND

5

MOUNT RAINIER NATIONAL PARK

Tacoma

NISQUALLY REACH

FORT LEWIS

Olympia

NISQUALLY RIVER

TAHOMA

AREA OF MAP

NATIONAL FOREST

0   10
miles

ALDER DAM

SYLVAIN

below the dams may have prevented salmon from penetrating that high into the upper watershed. But dams can kill salmon by means other than barricading their migration journeys, and there is no doubt about the impacts of Alder Dam.

Alder delivered "peaking power" to Tacoma — that is, it released surges of water through the turbines to meet peak demands for electricity in the early mornings and late afternoons. The effects were felt all the way down the Nisqually River to the Delta. Unnaturally high flows from the peaks drove the salmon down to the bottom, disrupting their migration. Unnaturally low flows, when water was being held back, exposed spawning beds and created crowded, depleted pools where insufficient oxygen killed or weakened the salmon. As for the Indian fishermen, they were driven off the river by the peaking-power surges. As Billy puts it, "We knew when they were coming, and we just got the hell off the river rather than fight the high water."

The impacts of the Centralia Dam and canal were even worse.

When I went to the dam site and hiked the canal in early September 1997, it was easy to see how the operation had stressed the river. The water in the canal moved along at a brisk pace, while the Nisqually itself, lacking more than half of its natural flow for a full fourteen river miles, ran low and sluggish. But, even though the river is still plainly paying a price today, my visit took place after the Tribe's grueling campaign to repair the river. In 1977, when Billy laid out his plan for the Nisqually, Centralia's project had not yet been modified and the river was anything from a dry bed to a trickle for most of the summer and early fall between the Centralia power plant and dam. Those few fish that could get through confronted the six-foot dam, although by then it had a poorly functioning fish ladder.

Development, especially after World War II, brought other problems to the river. The Forest Service, which administers 10 percent of the land in the Nisqually watershed, jacked up the timber cut after 1945. So did Weyerhaeuser and the other timber companies that own a total of 18 percent of the land. The resulting erosion silted over spawning beds and clouded the river. The aggressive logging, along with other development, changed the run-off pattern. In addition, the fish faced new enemies in the form of herbicides and pesticides.

By the 1970s the biggest and best fish, the wild spring chinook, had gone nearly extinct, as had the fall run of chum. The numbers of fall chinook, coho, pink, and steelhead all were way down. The only healthy run left was the winter run of chum bound for Muck Creek. A few years before Billy Frank sent his 1977 memorandum to the Nisqually people, the Washington Department of Fisheries had called the Nisqually watershed "one of the most striking examples of the encroachment of civilization on a river basin and the resultant depletion of river runs of food fish."

In the 1977 memo (the ideas were Billy's, but pen was put to paper by the adroit hand of Hank Adams), Billy set out a clear objective and an approach to achieve it. The primary goal was to enhance the Nisqually fishery "to provide equitable fishing incomes or a livelihood to at least 100 tribal fishermen. . . ." This was a bold objective: at the time, only a handful of Nisqually were able to make a living as fishermen. The tribal plan had three main strategies: reducing the destructive effects of the Tacoma and Centralia dams; developing a sophisticated tribal fisheries program, including two tribal hatcheries; and

reducing the interception of fish bound for the Nisqually River, with priority on treaty negotiations between the United States and Canada.

The Nisqually Tribe had already filed two legal actions against the cities of Tacoma and Centralia. The Federal Energy Regulatory Commission (FERC) has authority to license hydroelectric dams on navigable rivers. The Tribe had invoked the jurisdiction of FERC (originally the Federal Power Commission) in hopes of obtaining orders that would alter the dam operations to protect the salmon. Although the Tribe had filed the initial petitions in 1975, the proceedings would not formally be brought to a close until 1993.

The cases were assigned to Administrative Law Judge Stephen Grossman. FERC proceedings are complex and, for all practical purposes, they amount to trials in federal district court. The cases are heard in federal courtrooms or formal FERC hearing rooms, the judges wear robes, and the place is crawling with lawyers. The hearings proceed according to the Federal Rules of Evidence. When he is off the bench, Judge Grossman is genial and relaxed, but in his courtroom he runs a tight ship.

There is no doubt that these cases, Billy Frank, and the Nisqually River made a lasting impression on Judge Grossman. He could see from the beginning that the proceedings would be out of the ordinary. The initial hearing was set for Judge George Boldt's courtroom in Tacoma and, due to fear for Judge Grossman's safety, Judge Boldt assigned two U.S. Marshals to protect him. Looking back on the protracted cases, Judge Grossman reflected that "it was sort of like doing God's work. All I was was a facilitator, although I had more power than most. As soon as the parties began to understand they had to work together, things began to happen."

Judge Grossman was on the leading edge of the judiciary. He believed in alternative dispute resolution, a term barely part of legal discourse in the 1970s. He told the parties (the Puyallup Tribe and two Washington state fish and wildlife agencies had joined the case as intervenors) that they knew far more about the river and its dams than he could ever know. They could fashion a workable system — a settlement — far better than he could. The parties, if they would cooperate, could find a way to operate the river for both salmon and power-production. Complex, multi-party litigation raising broad social issues was still new to our courts, and Judge Grossman was well ahead of his time in recognizing that comprehensive settlements, crafted by the parties themselves, had many advantages over litigating cases to the bitter end.

Of all the lawyers and the many others involved, Billy Frank best understood what Judge Grossman was getting at. "It was quite clear to me from the beginning that Billy understood the big picture. He could see beyond the parochial position of one party and could see the needs of the other parties. He knew that the parochial needs could be met through meeting the needs of the other parties. He was invaluable."

Billy was in it for the long haul, and he developed solid relationships with city officials, lawyers, and other decision-makers. "Billy was always there," Judge Grossman recounted. "I can't remember a single session when he wasn't there. He was the driving force. He never let anybody quit. I think he inherited that spirit from his father."

Certainly there was little to be encouraged about in the beginning. "At the start of the cases," Judge Grossman recalled, "the river was so devoid of fish that just a couple of

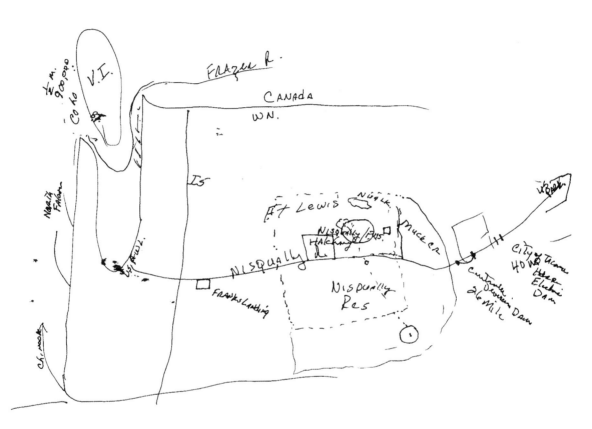

Maps or sketches are trademark to meals or meetings with Billy Frank. One friend calls him "the cartographer *par excellence*, diagrammist *extraordinaire*, and master mapmaker of the Nisqually Tribe." This drawing of salmon migration routes was penned on the back of a café placemat.

Nisqually fishermen could make a living out of it. There were just very few salmon. The releases from Alder and La Grande dams were a problem. The river from Centralia Dam to Centralia Powerhouse was a disaster."

By the late 1970s, however, the parties had made progress and most of them had agreed to an interim flow regime that substantially increased the amount of water in the river during the critical run times. But, because the fish must go out to the ocean and mature, it would take five years to find out whether the regime was working. In the fall of the fifth year, Judge Grossman ordered all the attorneys out to the river. By then, site visits to the Nisqually had become commonplace in the proceedings. This time they would see that their work was paying significant dividends.

Judge Grossman remembers the day well. "We all went out there at the beginning of the migration season, when the Nisqually had their religious catch. I made the attorneys show up at some ungodly hour, I think it was 6:00 a.m. There were more fish than anybody had seen in years. I made the lawyers help pull up the nets. It was very satisfying. There were tears in some people's eyes."

The cases had many other unorthodox moments. One of the issues was whether the Nisqually River was navigable under the Federal Power Act; otherwise, FERC would have no jurisdiction over Centralia's project. Billy's dad had ridden logs on the river and seen floats of shingle bolts down the river, all before the turn of the century. If proven, those activities would indicate navigability under the law.

But Billy's dad was more than a hundred years old, and the journey to the courtroom in Seattle would be hard on him. They could do his testimony by deposition, but Judge Grossman felt that it should be given in person. The evidence was important. Beyond that, the judge felt that he should hear the testimony directly, "out of respect for the old man."

So they packed up this major federal administrative proceeding and moved it down to Frank's Landing — right into Willie Frank, Sr.'s, little living room. The five lawyers, the judge, the observers, and the court reporter pecking away at the stenotype machine, all had trouble hearing the old man's words. He had even more trouble hearing theirs, and there were a good many hollered-out attorneys' questions. But Billy's dad told his story of the river, and the Ninth Circuit Court of Appeals upheld the finding that the Nisqually qualified as a navigable river.

Willie and Angeline Frank (1879–1983; 1891–1986) raised their son, Billy, along with Angeline's earlier children, Rose, Andrew, Maiselle, and Don. Shown here in 1981 at their Frank's Landing home, they could take great pride in their children and grandchildren — and in their own lives and legacy.

The proceedings officially came to an end in 1993, when Judge Grossman entered a formal termination order. In it, he included a paragraph rare for federal judicial proceedings:

> The resolution of this case is a tribute by all parties to the vision of Bill Frank, Sr., a Nisqually elder who, at the age of 104, testified in the Centralia jurisdictional hearing. Mr. Frank recalled the river's former majesty and importance to the Nisqually Tribe, and eloquently expressed his desire for restoration of that irreplaceable resource. Unfortunately, he died soon after that case concluded. His spirit and vision, however, live on in his son, Bill Frank, Jr., who has devoted his life to achieving cooperative solutions to Northwest fisheries disputes. . . . [Bill Frank, Jr.'s] extraordinary achievements were recognized in 1992 when he was awarded the Albert Schweitzer Prize for Humanitarianism.

The Schweitzer Prize is a prestigious international human rights honor, awarded by Johns Hopkins University and carrying an honorarium of $10,000. Recipients have included former President Jimmy Carter, former Surgeon General C. Everett Koop, and Norman Cousins.

I asked Judge Grossman whether he had written other tributes of this sort in his career, which encompasses some four or five hundred formal written opinions and orders. He responded, "No. I've never felt inclined to do it in another case. As a matter of fact, I've never even considered it. This was a very unusual case with very unusual parties. I thought it was appropriate. And I still think it was appropriate."

Altering the Nisqually's flow regime, important though it was, made up only part of the plan for restoring the river. So many runs had gone extinct or been decimated, and so much spawning habitat had been lost, that new or expanded fish hatcheries would be required to build up the salmon numbers.

Billy and the Tribe used the FERC proceedings as levers to put fish in the river. The settlement with Centralia was one step. In addition to installing a new fish ladder at the dam and new fish screens at the diversion canal, the city agreed to maintain two salmon-rearing ponds. Centralia also paid the

Tribe $3.2 million, to be used for tribal fisheries management. These funds are available for other fisheries enhancement and restoration projects, such as expanding and improving the Tribe's Kalama Creek Hatchery, constructed in 1977.

But Kalama Creek could not match Clear Creek, which, although only a half-mile long, is prime salmon-rearing habitat. The waters of Clear Creek are created by a "weeping bluff." This low cliff, which parallels the east bank of the lower Nisqually River, is a cornucopia for ocean-going fish: within a stretch of half a mile, two hundred small springs and five major ones flow out of the bluff and merge into Clear Creek. The water in this spring-fed creek is clean and clear and the perfect temperature for salmon — a warm 50 degrees in the winter, a cool 52 degrees in the summer. At river mile six, the site lay downstream of the Centralia facilities and would give the fish short, easy runs to and from Puget Sound: smolts could make it to saltwater in one day. Clear Creek was the best place in the Nisqually watershed for a major fish hatchery.

Except that Clear Creek and the weeping bluff, and all access routes to them, lay entirely within the Fort Lewis military reservation.

Military land or no, by the late 1970s Billy was determined to put Clear Creek land — which was, after all, former Nisqually reservation land — to its highest and best use. In 1979 Senator Warren Magnuson, who was deeply committed to improving the Northwest's fisheries, obtained a $1 million appropriation for the U.S. Fish and Wildlife Service to conduct a feasibility study for a hatchery at Clear Creek. Billy was joined in 1980 by George Walter, an anthropologist who had done field work to determine how the Nisqually River fishery, and the tribal members' relationship to it, had changed over time. The Tribe hired Walter, and eventually he became supervisor of the environmental program. Careful, knowledgeable, dedicated, and an astute strategist, he and Billy saw eye-to-eye from the beginning. Like Hank Adams and Jim Anderson (executive director of the Northwest Indian Fisheries Commission), George Walters became one of Billy's most trusted colleagues, a full partner in the sacred task of bringing back a river and its fish.

Billy and George approached the commanding general at Fort Lewis, who had doubts whether a tribal fish hatchery was a proper use of military land. The matter was at a standstill, but only temporarily. "I always try to work with people, to give them a chance," Billy says. "But sometimes you have to go over their heads."

Billy had close working relationships with Congressman Norm Dicks, who represented the district, and Senator Dan Evans. In 1983, Billy invited both men to come out and look at Clear Creek. By then, the matter of funding had been complicated by President Reagan's announced opposition to spending federal money on fish hatcheries. At the Clear Creek visit, Billy, George, and other tribal representatives explained the area's potential for salmon rearing and its rare suitability as a hatchery site. A magnificent spot, tucked away down by the river among big-leaf maple and 500-year-old fir and cedar, the site was clearly not essential to military purposes.

Evans and Dicks made some pointed calls to the Pentagon. Then they put through, without any opposition from the army or the White House, an appropriation to complete the feasibility study that Magnuson had initiated. To no one's surprise, the U.S. Fish and Wildlife Service concluded that Clear Creek was an optimum site for a fish-rearing facility. By the late 1980s, Congress had authorized funds for an $8.2 million hatchery, one of the largest in the State of Washington.

It would operate on 130 acres of military land, leased by the army to the Nisqually Tribe in perpetuity.

The federal funding provided only construction money, not operation and maintenance funds, but this never slowed down Billy Frank and George Walter, both of whom knew how to put together the pieces of a puzzle. In 1989 the Tribe formally settled its FERC suit against the City of Tacoma. The city agreed to operate Alder Dam to provide satisfactory instream flows for salmon and to cease using the facility for peaking-power. Tacoma also agreed to pay the Tribe a minimum of $435,000 annually for operation and maintenance of the Clear Creek Fish Hatchery.

The facility, with its state-of-the-art fisheries laboratory, opened in 1991. Each year it will produce up to 650,000 coho yearlings and 4 million fall chinook. Many are released in cold-water spawning beds in the upper watershed, including the Mashel River, one of the main tributaries for the once-thriving wild chinook. It is still too early to know how successful the hatchery will be, but the indications so far are good. The numbers of returning fish in the late 1990s have exceeded expectations and the chinook have been weighing up to a robust fifty pounds. The tribal operation on

The Clear Creek Hatchery opened on August 17, 1991. In 1918, the creek's pristine waters were taken from Nisqually Indians for World War I purposes. Restoring this ideal hatchery site to the Tribe has allowed a rebirth of chinook and silver salmon in abundance for the Nisqually watershed.

army land under the weeping bluff should be a major force in helping to restore silver life to the Nisqually.

Once I asked Billy what he thought when he heard the term "Fort Lewis." Did it make him sad? Did it make him bitter? What about the loss of land and family, of identity? Billy's answer, which he elaborated upon in several later discussions, told volumes about how, if social progress is to be made, a leader must keep ever focused on the ultimate objective and must transcend stereotypes, past transgressions, and even personal hurts of the most profound nature.

"It sure used to make me sad. And angry. You can say that the army was our enemy when they took our land on the other side of the river. Dad had to live that, and I grew up with it.

"Those weren't good times. But they aren't these times. These are different times. It has to do with the survival of a people.

"My blood doesn't boil any more. Some of those trees in there are 500 years old, some maybe a thousand. Nobody bothers them. Fort Lewis — the army — protects them.

"You have to understand their mission. The army's mission is to train troops, not to cut trees. We've had long talks with their generals and colonels about their mission and ours. Now they're an ally. The army is a much better land manager than the Forest Service.

"You can deal with the army. The commanding general is the boss. It's not like with the governor or the president or the Secretary of the Interior. When I talk to those guys, I don't know who the hell's in charge. But when I go across the river to Fort Lewis, I know who's in charge. When he tells his soldiers — 'Don't drive any more tanks across Muck Creek,' or 'Don't poison that lake anymore,' or 'Let those Indian people collect their medicines' — that's what's going to happen. Boy, that is powerful. When you've gotten a handshake with the General — Boy! It's been very positive over the past twenty years.

"Now I belong to the Officers' Club. Look, I'm no officer. How the hell do I belong to the Officers' Club? But I do.

"A few years ago the Northwest Indian Fisheries Commission couldn't find a golf course for its annual golf tournament. So I said, 'Hey, I belong to the Officers' Club.' The General said 'Sure!' when I asked him. I don't think they even charged us a fee.

"Now that's being neighbors. He knows we aren't going to do it every day. We know we can do it if we need it. That's being neighbors."

So today the army no longer aims its artillery at Muck Creek. The tanks no longer tear up riparian areas. A solid concrete bridge spans Muck Creek. The elders can use Fort Lewis lands to gather their medicines — teas, ferns, princes pine, and many others — and roots for their baskets. The army provides some downed cedar logs for making canoes. Tribal vehicles have passes for the entrance gates, to assure access to the hatchery. And the Tribe can get through to high officials if necessary. How? Breaking into a smile, Billy allows that "I've got the General's phone number in his helicopter."

These are important contacts for Billy, and not just because both Norman Schwartzkopf and Colin Powell used to be the commanding general at Fort Lewis. Beyond that, these are allies and neighbors.

"A while ago I had to fire a guy at the Fish Commission. You know, there are guys who can sign letters for me. They're supposed to be cleared through Jim Anderson or George Walter. This guy didn't understand that.

"So he wrote this letter talking about retired admirals, generals, colonels. Jesus Christ, he went crazy criticizing them. He just assumed that the army was somebody whose ass you kicked. He assumed I was a guy who wanted to beat up on the army.

"So I started getting calls. 'Jesus Christ, Bill. This isn't you!'

"So you bet I had to fire the guy. When you talk about trying to protect your Tribe's rights over twenty years or a lifetime, you have to be sure about what you say and what you do and how you carry yourself. And that involves giving people respect. These people are our neighbors, good ones. Who do you want there — the army, or a bunch of subdivisions?"

It is startling, then, to cast aside preconceptions, as Billy has, and look in an objective way at Fort Lewis' role in achieving land health in the Nisqually watershed. The military installation encompasses 60,000 acres, 12 percent of all land in the watershed, more than the 10 percent the Forest Service holds, more, in fact, than is held by any other single owner. Leaving aside the central base, Fort Lewis is almost all open space. When you come down from the north on Highway 7 and then Highway 507, you pass through the franchise-cluttered strips of south Tacoma and

Spanaway. Then, as you cross the northern edge of the Nisqually watershed, you break out into wide-open country. Fort Lewis land lies on both sides of the highway.

One day, I stood with Billy and George Walter on the broad Muck Creek prairie, and George observed, "You can see why we want Fort Lewis to be here. This is the only place like this on the I-5 corridor in Washington." Billy added, "A general's mission is to train troops. He makes some noise. Sometimes he shakes the ground. Our mission is to protect the environment, to protect the salmon, the trees."

Our discussion took place to a chorus in the background. Ka-*boom*. *Whump*. An occasional visible spray of soil flared in the Impact Area at the far end of the prairie, where artillery shelling is allowed. Wha-*boom. Blomp.* It makes one realize the difference between wilderness, which this is not, and wildlife habitat, which, except for parts of the Impact Area (which does not affect Muck Creek or the main-stem Nisqually), this most definitely is. Discordant though it may sound, Fort Lewis provides better salmon habitat than the Forest Service. In the watershed, only Mount Rainier National Park at the high end, and the Nisqually National Wildlife Refuge at the Delta, assure superior habitat — and Fort Lewis is half again as large as those two areas combined.

None of which is to deny the surreal atmosphere of Fort Lewis.

In the early days of the FERC proceedings, Judge Grossman was conducting one of his portable federal administrative hearings. The judge and the lawyers came up the river by boat for a site visit. The Tribe had arranged a lunch, complete with frybread, salmon cooked the traditional way on racks over an open alder fire, and huckleberry pie. In the middle of lunch, the assembled party heard a massive grinding and crunching. It was the army, running practice maneuvers — the soldiers, decked out in fatigues, wearing green face paint, and adorned with leaves in their helmets, were laying out a pontoon bridge across the Nisqually River. The warriors were not for a moment dissuaded by the judge's firm but jocular court order: "You're interfering with an official federal judicial picnic!" For the next hour they stalked the picnickers, leaping gingerly from tree to tree and seeking cover behind parked cars and peeking out from behind the tires. Finally, when the court proceeding packed up and the threat to national security had subsided, the troops returned to the base.

Several ancient Nisqually prairies are now part of Fort Lewis (U.S. Army), where birdhouses, many built by students at Wa He Lut Indian School, are placed upon the native Garry oaks to restore populations of bluebirds.

George Walter, in addition to his many years of work to bring back the salmon, also has brought back the western bluebirds. They nest in cavities of old-growth trees and had been driven out when logging took most of the old trees on the lower Nisqually. Over time, George has built and installed 400 bluebird boxes, nailed to the sides of smaller trees, to replicate the cavities. One of my sweetest moments was standing next to George while he was at work on military land with the blessing of an official army pass. He opened up one of his bluebird boxes. "Looks like five babies.

This is the second brood this year for this pair. The first brood also had five." Then, patiently, gently, he held the little balls of blue and orange in his hands and placed thin aluminum bands on their tiny legs with a pair of needle-nosed pliers. When the moment passed, the ironic background chorus played its way back into my consciousness. *Blump.* Wha-*boom*.

The Nisqually Indian Reservation lies directly between what was formerly Fort Lewis' artillery launching facility on the west bank of the Nisqually and the Impact Area across the river. The launching facility was finally moved in the 1970s, but Billy just shakes his head at some of the memories. "You could hear those shells whistle on their way. You never could be sure exactly where the hell they would land. Once one landed right next to one of our fireworks stands and a big goddam fire broke out."

Nonetheless, over the course of a generation, the army made accommodations in favor of the Tribe, the river, and the salmon. All the long while, Billy hewed to his rules. Be patient. Keep a wide-open mind. Understand the other side's mission. Be consistent. Show respect. Make progress for the land and the fish and the people.

There is much more work to be done on the Nisqually. The problems of logging and agricultural pollution remain slow in their resolution. One area of progress has been the Timber/Fish/Wildlife Agreement (T/F/W), in which Billy played a central role. Negotiated among state forestry officials, the timber industry, the tribes, and environmentalists, the T/F/W process resulted in a consensus agreement over state forestry regulations applying to private lands.

On matters of land use generally, several grass-roots organizations have grown up and the Nisqually watershed has become a model of progress through citizen cooperation. Notable among the citizen organizations are the Nisqually River Basin Land Trust (of which George Walter is president), the Nisqually River Council, and the Nisqually River Education Project. They work steadily on a variety of education projects, habitat restoration efforts, and acquisitions of land and conservation easements. As vivid symbolism, the three groups share the same logo.

The Nisqually Tribe continues to play a leadership role. In 1999 the Tribe acquired the 410-acre Braget farm on the Delta, the last private holding within the Nisqually National Wildlife Refuge. The Tribe plans to breach the dikes, which had made the area suitable for farming, and allow saltwater to reclaim up to180 acres (the remainder of the Braget parcel is either upland or already marshland). The salmon that will benefit most are the young smolts. When making the transition from fresh to saltwater, the smolts eat macro-invertebrates — larval insects that dwell on or under rocks and mud. The breaching of the dikes, by allowing the farmland once again to become a salt flat, will thus create both more space and a greater food supply for the young salmon.

In the 1970s the Nisqually River was in great trouble. Today it is a river on the mend, a place to which people look as a standard for successful river restoration. The Delta, now a national wildlife refuge, has been called "the last unspoiled major estuary in Washington state," and "some of the most magnificent wetlands in the world." There was not, nor could there have been, any single lightning-bolt event that sparked restoration of the Delta and the Nisqually River. Instead, time after time, steady as the seasons, people have acted with dedication, constancy, and respect for the land and one another. These words can be truisms, but they also describe human qualities that foster land health in a way that nothing else can.

The Nisqually Delta's estuary marshes were diked and converted into prime dairy land early in the 20th century. In 1978, the homestead Brown farm (upper left) and Braget's farm (middle left) became the principal base for a new Nisqually National Wildlife Refuge. Anderson Island (top) was once a traditional Nisqually summer village site for shellfish harvesting and salmon curing. Frank's Landing (not shown) is a stone's throw from the upriver interstate freeway bridge (lower left).

CHAPTER 5

WA HE LUT

When we look at these events in the Nisqually watershed, we can gain some hope, quite a sizable measure of it, about how to achieve land health. Yet there is another perspective from which to view this river and green countryside at the southernmost end of Puget Sound. And from this vantage point, the Indian experience, the Indian values, the Indian world view become ever more relevant in addressing the current and future health of our landscapes — not just in the Nisqually watershed, but far beyond.

One way to assess land health is to compare a natural area, such as a watershed, with other similar areas. The Nisqually stands out in bold relief against most other watersheds, especially those with large-scale urban and industrial development, which the Nisqually does not have. Conservationist Aldo Leopold, however, used a different benchmark. In *A Sand County Almanac*, he wrote that one of the fundamental values of wilderness is to give us a point of departure: "A science of land health needs, first of all, a base datum of normality, a picture of how healthy land maintains itself as an organism." We need to measure degraded land against what it once was. Otherwise, we lose our collective memory and our will to act is dulled.

Billy Frank, Jr., speaks of the same idea. "I see the changes from my dad's time to my time, to the time of my kids and grandkids. How much can western Washington, Puget Sound, take of people? I worry about children seeing a creek or a river that is dry. Maybe they think that's what a river is, a dry bed. I want them to see the birds flying, the killer whales out there, everything that swims. I want them to see the big ant piles under the fir trees, to see the soft, protected soils they make. Now the only place you can see those ant piles is up on the military land. All these things are signs, measurements."

These comparisons are not easy to make. The state of land health that Aldo Leopold and Billy Frank refer to has never been static. The river has changed the landscape with every big-water flood. We know that the Nisqually used controlled burns to bring up the prairie vegetables in the spring. Beyond that, our data, our measurements, are imperfect. We have an incomplete picture of the landscape before the Indians had contact with Europeans.

Still, there is much we do know, and when we piece the changes together — comparing the Nisqually watershed's current land health with the early 1800s rather than with today's developed watersheds on Puget Sound — the results are daunting, disturbing.

In 1844 James McAllister (who would later lose his life in the United States–Nisqually conflict) established his farm. The valley continued to attract agriculturists. The Brown farm, one of the largest, began its operations on the Delta in 1904. Alson Brown — in order to accommodate 300 milking cows, 20,000 chickens, and 1,200 to 2,000 hogs yearly, not to mention a hotel sleeping fifty — diked much of the Delta to keep the saltwater out and create arable land. Although the Tribe is breaching the Braget farm dikes, the dikes constructed by the Brown farm still stand, keeping the Delta — wonderland though it is to our eyes — far from its natural, marshy state.

Sheepherders grazed their animals on the Nisqually prairies. Billy's dad witnessed the results. The overgrazing took out most of the native carrots,

potatoes, and onions. "The sheep destroyed all the roots. They left nothing."

Today numerous farming operations lie in the flood plain, and rain and floods wash large amounts of animal wastes into the river. As the Nisqually River Management Plan, prepared by the Nisqually River Task Force and the Washington Department of Ecology, explains: "The cumulative effects of approximately thirty dairies, plus numerous vegetable farms, chicken farms, and hobby farms in the basin [create] a high potential for local surface and ground water pollution." Fecal coliform levels sometimes exceed regulatory limits. Because of this, the Washington Department of Health has declared that the shoreline off the mouth of the Nisqually must be closed to commercial shellfish harvesting for five days following any rainfall of one-half inch or more. Remember: Billy Frank's generation, and the Nisqually people for hundreds of generations before him, once drank out of this river.

By the turn of the century, logging surpassed farming as the top economic producer in the watershed. Frederick Weyerhaeuser put together an empire in the Cascades. He built its foundation by buying up Northern

Pacific Railroad holdings, but he was interested in any ground stocked with virgin timber. "The only mistake I have made," Weyerhaeuser was fond of saying, "is not buying timber when it was offered to me."

The early accounts all mention the thick, tall stands of fir and cedar that came right down to the shoreline. Timber companies, with Weyerhaeuser leading the way, acquired more than 18 percent of the Nisqually watershed. The low-lying, private lands were harvested first. Then, after World War II, the cutting moved into the higher, more rugged national forests. Today, outside of some stands in Fort Lewis and Mount Rainier National Park, the ancient forests in the watershed are gone. Logging of national forest land continues, although the harvest has come down significantly and clearcutting is used sparingly. On private lands, however, clearcuts still take out broad swaths of second-growth stands on the slopes of the upper Nisqually. Billy minces no words about the impact of intensive logging on the watershed. "We get these big floods. What do you expect when there aren't any big trees up there to hold back the water? What do you expect from all the damn roads they've cut in up there?"

Most animal species no longer find the Nisqually watershed as welcoming as once it was. The deer and elk are an exception, because intensive logging has created the kind of forest openings these grazing ungulates favor. Eagles are increasing — as of the late 1990s there were twelve nesting pairs — but they remain far below their historic numbers. In all, eleven plant species and sixteen animal species in the watershed are classified by federal or state agencies as endangered, threatened, or sensitive. Mount Rainier National Park, which protects the Nisqually headwaters, has lost five to seven species of large mammals over the past thirty to forty years. Black bears, cougars, and lynx — objects of a relentless bounty hunting program begun in 1865 and continuing for a century — are certainly well below historic levels. The king of the mountains, the grizzly bear, is long gone. The sporadic reports of the wolf's piercing call remain unconfirmed.

Out on the Delta and Nisqually Reach, the birds are below historic numbers, but it is impossible to say by how far. The white swans Billy so loved as a boy hardly ever come back. The flounders he used to scare up with his bare feet are less numerous. Fewer gray whales come through, and numbers of them have washed up on the beaches. Biologists speculate that one problem may be lack of food. "The forest under the water — like the one we can see up on the sides of the mountain — is dying. No one sees that forest, but it's dying."

The ironies and complexities were spread out in front of me on a summer day. Billy and I were talking in his boat, drifting easily just off the mouth of the river. We had as companions more than one hundred harbor seals. At first they spooked, but after an hour they grew accustomed to their intruders. Eventually they surrounded us, some lying or plopping along on the shore, most of them diving and feeding in the open water. We reveled in the action, laughing at the slapping, honking, splashing, snorting, and squawking. "Jesus Christ!" Billy exclaimed. "Aren't they wonderful!" Later, as we got ready to shove off, he grew serious. "You know, back then there wouldn't be so many seals crowded in here. The salmon were plentiful and the seals would be all over the Sound. Now they have to group together at the mouth of the river. The seals are part of this. We've got to be sure to put some salmon aside for them."

And what aspect of the natural world could be more central to defining the Nisqually watershed than the salmon? The spring run of chinook is gone, or nearly so. The wild fall run is barely hanging on. The chinook runs from the Clear Creek Fish Hatchery are new, just a few years old, and must still be considered fragile. Only a few steelhead straggle up the river. The wild coho is virtually gone and the hatchery production is way down. No one knows why. It may well be that even the adjusted flow regime is inadequate for the coho. Only the Muck Creek chum salmon runs remain strong, but chum is the least desirable species from a commercial standpoint.

"Our fishermen still get only 10¢ a pound for the chum. The pen-fed fish from aquaculture are killing us. They'll ship you any size you want [holding his hands twelve inches, then eighteen inches, then two feet apart], and they'll ship it to you by air wherever you are. You want it in your restaurant or your grocery store tomorrow morning, and you'll have it. They're even bringing in those farm fish from Chile."

Billy homed in on the problem of habitat. "We're losing the things that make a healthy river — the rotting trees, the rotting fish. Remember that big old downed maple that shaded and sheltered the eddy and the salmon when I first got arrested back in '45? Most of that kind of stuff is gone, cleared away. Now we have siltation from the clearcuts. And then there's all the construction.

"Pretend you're a salmon. You're in Elliott Bay. 'Hey, it's not like it was seven years ago. What the hell are these pylons I'm having to swim around? This water seems oily.' Then you go into your river. You're swimming along, trying to find your way. 'My stream's dry! Where's my home? Where's that stream I came from?'

"Or, 'God*dam*, what the hell is this dam? It wasn't here seven years ago. What do I do now?'

"That salmon has to go back to its original stream. There are ways they can adapt to Mount St. Helens, but this is tougher.

"I try to tell people what I saw on our river fifty and sixty years ago. Now the river's basically shut down. It's hit the low end. And now we're trying to bring it back. But I'll tell you, it's hard."

The Nisqually watershed stands as an emblem of our species' shared predicament. The Nisqually: a great national park at its head; a great national refuge at its mouth. The object of a visionary restoration effort. Pristine. Just look at all the other Puget Sound river systems. And then look again. The Nisqually: the water, forests, and prairies reworked and redefined; the chaotic free play of nature tamed, diluted, tainted, and debased. More people are on the way.

It is worthwhile to mark the extraordinary exertions, of which the Nisqually watershed restoration is but one example, of Indian people to resuscitate natural systems. Indian leaders helped to negotiate the 1985 United States–Canada Salmon Treaty and have continued to play leadership roles in the complex and thorny fisheries issues with Canada. In the early 1990s a delegation, led by Billy Frank and Congresswoman Jolene Unsoeld, met with Third World U.N.

A 1991 editorial cartoon signifies the public prominence attained by Billy Frank in addressing major Northwest issues. Pulitzer Prize–winner David Horsey's imagery reflects the vivid word pictures characteristic of Billy's animated speech.

They talk about cheap electricity. Hydropower. It's not cheap. It's all been paid for by the salmon. When these lights come on, a salmon comes flying out.

▶ Billy Frank, Jr. Nisqually Tribe

©1991 SEATTLE POST-INTELLIGENCER

delegations and swung key votes to outlaw the "Curtains of Death" — the high-seas gillnets, up to forty miles long, that big ocean trawlers employed to capture every fish (and turtle, bird, and dolphin) of any size within their imposing sweeps. A conversation between Billy and the head of the Washington Forest Products Association sparked the negotiations leading to the Timber/Fish/Wildlife agreement, the consensus effort among the state, industry, tribes, and environmentalists which set state forestry regulations for timber harvesting on private lands. The Chelan Agreement of 1990, which has yet to prove out as well as T/F/W, was a consensus effort to develop comprehensive water planning to protect fish and wildlife from water withdrawals. In 1997 Washington tribes played a key role in the Tribal Rights–Endangered Species Joint Secretarial Order, which will give deference to tribal resource management when federal officials administer the Endangered Species Act.

The flagship natural resource organization for Washington tribes is the Northwest Indian Fisheries Commission, a project of nineteen Puget Sound and Olympic Peninsula tribes. Today, the Commission has a staff of sixty, with fifty professionals,

Billy Frank presented his issues to Bill Clinton in 1992. At his 1995 Pacific Rim Economic Conference, the President joked: "I've sat you next to Alice Rivlin (Budget Director), Billy, because I know you and the salmon need the money."

including biologists, ecologists, computer modelers, policy analysts, and lawyers. The Commission's wide-ranging work includes cutting-edge laboratory and field research in fish genetics and fish health. As reminders of the Commission's roots, the walls of its Olympia headquarters are adorned with large black-and-white photographs of the resisting Indian fishermen during the 1960s and 1970s.

Billy has served as the Commission's chair since 1977, except for one brief respite. ("We were going to rotate it, and after a while Dale Johnson from Makah took over for two years and he said 'The hell with this,' so it came back to me.") The Commission has gone a long way to fulfill the dreams of the 1970s: that the Boldt decision, along with expert tribal management, would not only defuse the conflict and violence between Indians and non-Indians but could, as well, use Indian treaty rights as a lever for improving the runs — and the habitat — for all fishers.

The tribes all have their own natural resource departments. The Nisqually, one of the smaller tribes, has an on-reservation staff of thirty. In total, considering both the Commission and the individual tribes, Washington Indian tribes employ some 200 fisheries scientists. Extraordinarily, this exceeds the number of fisheries scientists employed by the State of Washington and is apparently more than half the number of federal fisheries scientists in the state. Tom Laurie, of the Washington Department of Ecology, emphasizes the constructive role of tribal fisheries manage-

ment. The Boldt decision and the resultant rise in tribal fisheries scientists, he believes, signaled a "rebirth of the profession. Before then, the state was going along unchecked. The Boldt decision gave science a central role. Suddenly, the quality of science mattered." Laurie also notes, as have many others, that the fisheries staffs on the reservations give the tribes a greater presence out in the watersheds than that of either the state or federal governments. And the tribes have persevered. "There was a time," Laurie recalls, "when people expected tribes to have short-lived professional staffs. But the staffs have stayed, and stayed committed."

The tribal movement toward professional resource management is all the more remarkable when we recall the situation in Indian Country just a generation ago. In the mid-1970s few tribes had any natural resources departments at all, and if they did, the staffs were skeletal, consisting of just a few employees. What would be the condition of our lands and waters if the federal and state governments were willing to commit such a large percentage of their financial resources to natural resources management?

Maiselle Bridges led a restoration of the Puyallup Tribe to prominence and vitality under the Medicine Creek Treaty. Her role at Frank's Landing is equally legendary. The Wa He Lut Indian School is hallmark to her heart and life.

The revival of American Indian tribalism in this country over the past two generations has necessarily involved social activism, court cases, negotiations with the federal and state governments, and the building of tribal governmental agencies and programs. Coursing through all of these developments has been the Indian way, and the individual and tribal tenacity to keep it alive and allow it to flourish.

"Not so long ago we had our culture and our ceremonies intact. Then the white man came with his wars and his legislation, which was just another kind of war. Here's how I think of the Indian. He's running from the army. He fights. He runs and he fights again. He's tired. He's losing his people to war, disease. The white man is passing laws saying he can't do his ceremonies and dances, he can't speak his language. Then he stops running and fighting and he says, 'For us to survive, we have to do something different. I better save what I still have.' So he bows down and finds ways to adjust. But he's never going to let his culture die. He's just going to have to do things differently."

Billy's sister, Maiselle Bridges, did it differently. Instead of the state or federal schools, she wanted to have a true Indian school for Indian children. In 1974 she founded an Indian school

at Frank's Landing and named it after Wa He Lut, Leschi's lieutenant, who lived until long after the Leschi War and remained steadfastly loyal to Leschi and his spirit.

Wa He Lut Indian School, grades K through 9, educates Indian children in the southern Puget Sound area, without any tuition from parents. It is funded mostly by federal grants and support from the smoke shop at the Frank's Landing Indian Community. Maiselle remains its guiding light, and her daughters, Alison and Suzette, serve on its board. Billy and Hank

Cedar totem poles, relating ancient myths in symbols carved by 80-year-old Simon Charlie, continue traditions for Wa He Lut Indian School. The $4 million building replaces structures lost to a 1996 flood. Its classrooms can serve 130 students in kindergarten through 9th grade.

Adams work on keeping the funding secure. The original school building was destroyed by the raging high waters of the flood of February 1996, but a striking new structure has now been completed on the same site.

The Indian way, including its ties to the natural world, is alive and well at Wa He Lut. One teacher told me, "You see the same thing here as in the school I taught in at Navajo. The kids with the most Indian culture cause the fewest disciplinary problems. They're the most anchored. Wa He Lut allows kids with the traditions to keep them and kids without much tradition to acquire more." The ideal is to integrate cultural traditions seamlessly into the educational process, without in some way proselytizing. And, to my eye, seeing it in practice, that is how it works. In the fourth grade class at Wa He Lut, for example, just as with my son Ben's elementary school class in Boulder, the teacher calls the students together for circle. But she does this by tapping on a drum. She reads a story about an Indian boy going fishing and catching a large fish. The class goes out huckleberry picking in the fall. They use willows to build a sweat lodge and gather cattails and weave mats for the lodge's floor. The students are recording Indian languages. Wa He Lut students have constructed nesting boxes, similar to those that George Walter uses to bring back the bluebirds.

The new Wa He Lut school building for Indian children at Frank's Landing is brightened by abundant Indian arts and crafts — and by history, real history. In 1980, on Billy's birthday, after the Fish Wars had finally ended when the United States Supreme Court affirmed the Boldt decision, state game wardens

Students at Wa He Lut Indian School frolic on a playground climber for a 1976 yearbook photo. Frank's Landing families founded Wa He Lut in 1974. A next generation of children now attend Wa He Lut in the new school that opened in 1998.

returned the canoe that they had confiscated in 1964. Johnny Bobb's graceful handiwork in cedar, a full twenty-five feet in length, along with Billy's carved paddle, hang from the ceiling at Wa He Lut.

The founding of Wa He Lut School, the refusal to relinquish the right to fish despite the state's exertions, the restoration of the Nisqually watershed, and the work of the Northwest Indian Fisheries Commission all reflect a distinctive way of seeing the world. I can say without hesitation that few things I have been blessed to experience have moved or inspired me as much as the struggle of Indian people to endure as peoples. And endure they have. It is in this sense that Billy Frank's legacy is not in his accomplishments as an individual but rather in his active and purposeful embodiment of a world view.

"The white people haven't cared about the river. Nobody along this river cared that there was a river here. All they thought was 'I can dam it or divert it or drain it.' 'I can make money off this river.'

"When the Indian takes a fish he makes an offering. He has respect for

the fish. When he wrestles a big salmon into the boat and then it gets away, he doesn't get angry. 'Well, it wasn't his time to come in here. It was his time to go up the river.'

"When he takes an elk or a deer, he makes an offering. It may be some ceremony he does, or it may just be thinking to himself about his appreciation for the elk and the forests it lives in. I've talked to Indians from other tribes. They do the same thing. The Indian doesn't take all the elk. He doesn't shoot him for his horns or as a trophy. He doesn't waste him. He does it to use the elk. He knows that the elk and the salmon run in his blood.

"We have ceremonies for the first salmon of each run. We bring everybody together and share the first salmon, and we train our children that way. When we eat the salmon we give our offerings to the fish and the river. We're not separate from the river. Indian people don't have a cathedral. We have the land and the river."

As a lawyer, I once believed that law could change the world. I no longer think of it that way. The world changes only as new ethics, philosophies, and world views change, evolve, and mature. Then the laws change to reflect the new ethics.

Perhaps in creating a new ethic toward the land, which is what we must do, we can look in a serious way to the Indian world view as personified in Billy Frank. People may say, "I'm not an Indian, that has no relevance to me." Yet we study Locke and Rousseau, as we should, even though seventeenth-century England and France in the Age of Reason are societies far removed from our own. We study Socrates and Lao-Tzu, though the cultures of Ancient Greece and China are distant and different from ours. We do not reject them. Instead, we take what is universal and valuable about their work and apply it to our own circumstances as we search for navigational stars in turbulent times.

Of any body of thought I know, the Indian world view holds the most sophisticated connection between our species and the natural world. Hardly primitive, it is in fact premised on what we now call "biodiversity" and "biocentricism." It is holistic. And it is based on reverence, and love, for the land.

Great Anglo thinkers have worked hard and well on these issues. Henry David Thoreau began his essay "Walking" with the passage: "I wish to speak a word for Nature, for absolute freedom and wildness, as contrasted with a freedom and culture

"It takes 500 years to grow a cedar to make a great canoe, so we can't destroy our forests," said Billy Frank in 1992. "We can't condemn our canoes to short lives, either." His warrior canoe continues life as an honored teacher, aloft on the cedar pole supports of the Wa He Lut Indian School atrium. Carved by aged Johnny Bobb as a gift for his young friend, it was seized by the state in 1964 and returned to Billy for his 60th birthday.

merely civil, — to regard man as an inhabitant, or a part and parcel of Nature, rather than as a member of a society." John Muir believed that "everything is connected by a thousand invisible cords." Edward O. Wilson has written of what he calls "biophilia," the call of nature that is an organic part of our humanity; Wilson's biophilia hypothesis, one writer explained, "proclaims a human dependence on nature that extends far beyond the simple issues of material and physical sustenance to encompass as well the human craving for aesthetic, intellectual, cognitive, and even spiritual meaning and satisfaction." Wallace Stegner thought of the animals on the Saskatchewan plains of his youth as his "little brothers and sisters." Aldo Leopold, in *A Sand County Almanac*, set out his land ethic, a full and fine philosophy based on the idea that humans are part of the natural world: "In short, a land ethic changes the role of *Homo sapiens* from conqueror of the land-community to plain member of it. It implies respect for his fellow-members, and also respect for the community as such."

But not one of these people, to whose values I also subscribe, has gone as deeply into nature as has the Indian world view. An equality with the natural world, an actual belonging to the same community, is in the bloodstream of Indian people. And they applied their philosophy. They learned how to live sustainably. And they did it here, in the American West. The Indians of the Northwest, Billy's fish people, have been here for at least 12,000 years. Six hundred generations of people living along the rivers and on the open and giving prairies, like the one along Muck Creek.

The ceremonies are critical to this, for ceremony, to which non-Indian conservationists have given scant attention, helps define and reaffirm who we are, what we stand for. Indian ceremonies celebrate the land and water and creatures and express a unity with, and commitment to, the natural world.

Ceremony, too, has a calming, bonding effect. It need not be an elaborate, day-long event. It can be a private, highly personal show of respect and honor, and it can be spontaneous, just a wave of support to a blue heron working the mud flats, a round of applause for late summer's first huckleberries, or "thank you" spoken into the water noises of your river.

Again, most of us do not live in

an Indian society. We need not, and could not, adopt the first salmon ceremony. But, recognizing the sophistication of the Indian world view and its pervasive spirituality, we could consider deepening our commitment to the Earth in the spirit of the first salmon ceremony. We could revere the natural world. We could think of ourselves not as giants but as equals with the runs and herds and packs and groves whose existence is so fragile because of us.

There is a profundity in the way Billy thinks about this. Why is it that we should feel an obligation to save some salmon for the seals and to preserve the big ant piles under the old-growth fir trees? "We talk about state sovereignty and tribal sovereignty, but those ant communities under the big fir trees are sovereign, too. We've got to find a way to protect *their* sovereignty." On another occasion he took it a step further. "It used to be, when I was a little boy, that we could see the stars at night. Now it's much

harder to see them, with all the lights from all the cities and towns. Some nights you can't see the stars at all. That's wrong. Those stars are sovereign. They have a right to be seen."

Doing all of this would be so hard for us to do. Hard for you, surely hard for me. The Indian world view is not only sophisticated, it is demanding. We would need to take emotional and intellectual chances, and it would take a great deal of time. Family, place, reverence, and ceremony just plain take time. I hope I can, in my own way, adopt some of it. I hope my sons will. I hope all of us will examine it for its universal value and its practical use.

"I don't believe in magic. I believe in the sun and the stars, the water, the tides, the floods, the owls, the hawks flying, the river running, the wind talking. They're measurements. They tell us how healthy things are. How healthy we are. Because we and they are the same. That's what I believe in."

Billy Frank with a harvest of fish in 1945, the year of his first arrest. "Those old carvers *engineered* those canoes. They made them so they had hardly any draft, just 6 or 8 inches. I could pole the canoe Johnny Bobb made me eight miles upstream. It didn't matter how shallow the riffles were. And a canoe had to be balanced just right. I've seen young kids learning to carve a canoe, put it in the water and — bang — just like that it'd tip over sideways and they'd be soaking wet. Of course, those canoes were beautiful, really graceful."

AFTERWORD

Putting together *Messages from Frank's Landing* has been one of the joys of my life. The best part has been my many hours of interviews with Billy, and the best of those were the easy, languid talks out on the River, the Sound, at Frank's Landing, and at the gracious home where Billy, Sue, and Willie live, overlooking the Nisqually Reach.

But another conversation with Billy also lies fresh in my mind. Not long ago, we had gone down to Albuquerque. Billy was the head, and I was a member, of a negotiating team on behalf of tribes. The idea was to create a special system for the federal administration of the Endangered Species Act with respect to tribal activities.

We had worked hard, negotiating with a group of top Interior and Commerce Department officials, from 9:00 a.m. straight through until about 9:30 in the evening. After a bracing dinner of Mexican food, our group went back to the hotel and talked into the night about the negotiations. We were tired but upbeat, because the effort was nearly over and it would make a very good agreement.

Billy and I went back up to my room a little after midnight. We talked for an hour or so. He was getting ready to go, and I asked a question that I'd wanted to ask Billy for a long time. "Billy are you hopeful? In the long run, can we save the wild salmon?"

He paused for a good minute. Then, sixty-five-years old, his tied-back hair streaked with gray, he leaned forward and answered, talking, as he always does, with his young-looking hands and his spirit as much as his voice:

"Here's what I tell Indian people when I talk to them. I tell them I wish we were managing thirty years before Judge Boldt issued his ruling in '74. I wish we had co-management then. We might have been able to use the treaties and our professionals back when we really needed it.

"But we do have that decision, and it gives us a chance. We're the advocates for the salmon, the animals, the birds, the water. We're the advocates for the food chain. We're an advocate for all of society. Tell them about our life. Put out the story of our lives, and how we live with the land, and how they're our neighbors. And how you have to respect your neighbors and work with your neighbors.

"So what you do is, you do what you can in your lifetime. Then that'll go on to another lifetime. Then another lifetime. Then another.

"Some of the scientists say that our river's spring chinook went extinct back in the '40s. I don't believe that. I *can't* believe that. That any salmon is extinct. The salmon was here when we got here. Nature put the salmon here. For us. And nature will take care of that salmon. That *life* is still here, in the streams, out in the ocean. I can't believe all that *life*, from the Nisqually headwaters all the way up to Alaska, is gone. I'll never say extinct. With a flicker of the right action, that life will revive itself."

Billy sat for a moment. Then he got up to leave and we gave each other bear hugs.

Tired, but too wound up to go to bed in spite of an early plane I needed to catch, I stayed up for a while, walking around the room in my rumpled clothes and my socks.

I realized how invested I've become in the question I'd asked him about hope. Young people ask me the same question with some frequency and urgency.

Look at what he's done, I kept saying to myself as I paced the room. Look at all he's done! And he's always been right before.

"*Billy!*" I found myself shouting it out loud, although he'd long been back in his room by now. "*Billy!* god*dam*mit, I'm sorry you've had to get a Social Security number, but I hope you live to a hundred and four!"

ACKNOWLEDGMENTS

I gained valuable information and advice from a great many people as I carried out the privilege of writing about the personalities and places that are the subject of this book.

Of course, the heart and soul of these pages come from my sixty hours of interviews with Billy Frank. I had known Billy for some twenty years, but had never had the chance to spend much one-on-one time with him. Nor did I fully appreciate the depth of the man. During our first interview, I took notes on what he said. I soon began writing down partial quotes. Then I reached a watershed moment: I realized that this would be his book, not mine — not only because this is his story but also because his philosophy, and the way he articulates it, are so rich, textured, and subtle. From that time on, I found myself acting nearly as a stenographer, taking down his words verbatim, regularly requiring him to repeat them, so that our readers could have as direct a line to him as possible.

So much of what we did was bathed in prodigious amounts of plain fun. One episode, from the summer of 1999, may give the flavor of my unusual kind of gratitude.

I had brought my nineteen-year-old son, Philip, out with me to the Puget Sound area on an interviewing trip. We wanted to travel by water with Billy from his home across the Nisqually Reach to the mouth of the river, and then go up the river to Frank's Landing. The tide was coming out, and about a quarter of a mile from the mouth of the river we ran aground on a sandbar lying a couple of feet below the surface. We leaped out of the vessel, hoping to dislodge it, but the tide was going out so fast that we had only a couple of minutes before the motorboat would be high and dry. We weren't quick enough. Low tide was still an hour and a half away, meaning that we had a wait of three hours before the water would return and lift us off.

Billy, of course, is nothing if not resourceful, so we did more than make do. "Come on, guys. Let's go!" For the next three hours, the three of us hiked around the mudflats — up to our calves in muck a good part of the way —

reveling in the fellowship, the sun, the birds, a few stray seals, the bracing smells of low tide, and the sweeping juxtaposition of water and land that makes up this part of southern Puget Sound. Time seemed to stop and wait for us as we conducted our sloppy, unorthodox, but thoroughly welcome hiking tour. Eventually, right on schedule ("You can always rely on the tide," Billy cheerfully advised Philip), the rising waters released our boat from the sandbar's embrace, and we were afloat once again.

Time was not all that waited for us. Also waiting — we were two hours late for a meeting — were friends at the Northwest Indian Fisheries Commission. No one was mad (just about everyone is long past getting mad at Billy), but there were quite a few barbed comments about the seamanship of a captain who would cause his craft and crew to become marooned, stranded.

Billy listened to the abuse for a while, waiting for it to subside. When it finally did, he spoke solemnly, concealing the belly laughs that would follow. He said simply, "We weren't marooned. [Pause.] And we weren't stranded. [Pause.] We were just temporarily delayed. [Pause.] And we had a hell of a lot more fun out on the Sound than you did back in this office."

Thank you, Billy, for everything. That covers a lot of ground — from tidal mudflats to the top of your mountain.

Sue Crystal, who has exquisite judgment, was an integral part of this book. She and what I call Billy's "Kitchen Cabinet" — Hank Adams, Jim Anderson, and George Walter — were always available for interviews, digging out documents and other information, reviewing manuscripts, and generally knocking around ideas. Lois Allen, Billy's assistant at the Fish Commission, did me more favors than I could ever count. I will always be in their debt.

Ralph Johnson, to whom this book is dedicated, was professor of law at the University of Washington and during his long and eminent career made immense contributions to the cause of Indian rights. Ralph died in September 1999 and did not live to see this book in print. Nonetheless, his wisdom and spirit live in these pages and carried me along as I wrote. What a great man.

Hank Adams selected the photographs (many from his own collection) and wrote the captions for them. Diane Sylvain, map maker for *High*

Country News, drew the maps. My thanks to both of them for their creativity.

Several research assistants dug up information through library work, interviews, and searches in agency files and on the web. For their fine work of that sort, as well as their many comments and suggestions, I give my gratitude to Scott Miller, Kevin Geiger, Andy Huff, Julia Miller, and Anna Ulrich.

My long-time faculty assistant, Cynthia Carter, was profoundly dedicated to *Messages from Frank's Landing* from the outset. She organized and coordinated research materials, scheduling, travel, and preparation of the manuscript. She is a careful, sophisticated, and talented reviewer. I shake my head at how much she matters to my work.

I was blessed by the colleagues who took the time to review the manuscript. This project would have been impossible without the expertise of Ralph Johnson, George Walter, David Getches, Bill Rodgers, Jim Anderson, and Cecelia Svinth Carpenter. Mrs. Carpenter, a historian and Nisqually tribal member, played a dual role: she both commented on several drafts and also produced a significant body of work on the history of the Nisqually Tribe, based in part on her many interviews with Nisqually elders, which was essential reading for me in writing this book.

Personal interviews were invaluable. I wish to thank, in addition to people already mentioned, Judge Stephen Grossman, Willard Hesselbart, Tiffany Johnson, Vivian Kendall, Fran Wilshusen, David Troutt, Tony Meyer, Sheila McCloud, Ron Olson, Terry Wright, Bruce Stewart, John Barr, Tom Laurie, David Harding, Howard Arnett, Elizabeth Furse, John Platt, Curtis Stanley, Richard White, Dick Trudell, Michael Taylor, Stan Humann, and Bruce Fortune. The staffs of several institutions were most cooperative in providing documents and other information; they include the Washington Department of Ecology, Washington Department of Health, Washington Department of Natural Resources, Washington Department of Fish and Wildlife, the Weyerhaeuser Company, Nisqually National Wildlife Refuge, Mount Rainier National Park, National Marine Fisheries Service, Fort Lewis, Wa He Lut Indian School, Nisqually River Basin Land Trust, Nisqually River Council, and Northwest Indian Fisheries Commission.

Messages from Frank's Landing,

although it has been revised and expanded since, was first presented at the University of Washington during two evening lectures, on November 18 and 19, 1997, as part of the Walker-Ames Lecture Series. It was a perfect forum in which to set out this material. I appreciate the hospitality of the University in general and Dean Roland Hjorth of the School of Law in particular. Earlier, I had expressed some of the notions here in the closing address at the 1997 Symposium on Western Lands at Oregon State University and in the 1996 Wallace Stegner Lecture at Montana State University, and I am appreciative for those opportunities to develop these ideas.

My own institution, the University of Colorado, continues to be a wonderful place to do my work. Hal Bruff, my dean, is a dear friend and never fails to encourage me on whatever trail I may choose. Chancellor Richard Byyny and Vice Chancellor Phil DiStefano have been most constructive in helping to create a welcoming environment for interdisciplinary work all across the campus.

Messages from Frank's Landing received a major boost late in the evening after I had given the first of the lectures in Seattle: I received a call from Pat Soden, director of the University of Washington Press, saying that he had been in the audience and thought this material might make a book the Press would like to publish. From that beginning, it was clear the Press was determined to give it a high priority, and in every step since, Pat and the Press have done what is needed to give honor to the Indian world view that is the essence of these messages from Frank's Landing.

Everyone in my family — Ann, Seth, Philip, Dave, and Ben — participated in some way in the writing of this book, and I thank them ever for their suggestions, support, and love. In this case, "family" also includes Bill, Sue, and Willie, who will always be in my heart. It includes, too, Anne Johnson, Ralph's wife. Ralph and Anne, whom I've known for a quarter of a century, were part of this book when I first imagined it, and remain so; among many other kindnesses, I stayed in their home on my interviewing trips out to Puget Sound and regularly talked the book through with them into the night. These messages arouse deep emotions, far more than I could have foreseen when I began, and family, variously defined, is an important part of them. And so I thank my family members for all the meaning they have brought into my life.

BIBLIOGRAPHY

BOOKS

Carl Abbott, *The Metropolitan Frontier: Cities in the Modern American West* (Tucson: University of Arizona Press, 1993).

American Friends Service Committee, *Uncommon Controversy: Fishing Rights of the Muckleshoot, Puyallup, and Nisqually Indians*, edited by Mary B. Isely and William Hanson (Seattle: University of Washington Press, 1970).

Mary W. Avery, *Washington: A History of the Evergreen State* (Seattle: University of Washington Press, 1961).

W. P. Bonney, *History of Pierce County, Washington* (Chicago: Pioneer Historical Publishing Co., 1927).

Bruce Brown, *Mountain in the Clouds: A Search for the Wild Salmon* (New York: Simon and Schuster, 1982).

Cecilia Svinth Carpenter, *Tears of Internment: The Indian History of Fox Island and the Puget Sound Indian War* (Tacoma, WA: Tahoma Research Service, 1996).

———, *Where the Waters Begin: The Traditional Nisqually Indian History of Mount Rainier* (Seattle: Northwest Interpretive Association, 1994).

———, *Leschi: Last Chief of the Nisquallies* (Orting, WA: Heritage Quest, 1986).

———, *Fort Nisqually: A Documented History of Indian and British Interaction* (Tacoma, WA: Tahoma Research Service, 1986).

Rachel Carson, *Silent Spring* (Greenwich, CT: Fawcett Publications, 1962).

Ella E. Clark, *Indian Legends of the Pacific Northwest* (Berkeley: University of California Press, 1953).

Fay G. Cohen, *Treaties on Trial: The Continuing Controversy over Northwest Indian Fishing Rights* (Seattle: University of Washington Press, 1986).

Felix S. Cohen, *Felix S. Cohen's Handbook of Federal Indian Law* (Charlottesville, VA: Michie Bobbs-Merrill, 1982 ed.).

Cecil Dryden, *Dryden's History of Washington* (Portland, OR: Binfords & Mort, 1968).

J. A. Eckrom, *Remembered Drums: A History of the Puget Sound Indian War* (Walla Walla, WA: Pioneer Press Books, 1989).

Robert E. Ficken and Charles P. LaWarne, *Washington: A Centennial History* (Seattle: University of Washington Press, 1988).

David H. Getches et al., *Cases and Materials on Federal Indian Law*, 3d ed. (St. Paul, MN: West Publishing Co., 1993).

David George Gordon, *Nisqually Watershed: Glacier To Delta — A River's Legacy* (Seattle: The Mountaineers, 1995).

Ralph W. Hidy et al., *Timber and Men* (New York: Macmillan, 1963).

Stephen R. Kellert and Edward O. Wilson, *The Biophilia Hypothesis* (Washington, DC: Island Press, 1993).

Arthur R. Kruckeberg, *The Natural History of Puget Sound Country* (Seattle: University of Washington Press, 1991).

Aldo Leopold, *A Sand County Almanac* (London: Oxford University Press, 1949).

Norbert MacDonald, *Distant Neighbors: A Comparative History of Seattle & Vancouver* (Lincoln: University of Nebraska Press, 1987).

Ezra Meeker, *Pioneer Reminiscences of Puget Sound: The Tragedy of Leschi* (Seattle: Lowman & Hanford, 1905).

———, *Seventy Years of Progress in Washington* (Seattle: n.p., 1921).

Murray Morgan, *Skid Road: An Informal Portrait of Seattle* (New York: Viking Press, 1951).

Gerald D. Nash, *The American West in the Twentieth Century: A Short History of an Urban Oasis* (Albuquerque: University of New Mexico Press, 1973).

Northwest Renewable Resources Center, *Building Bridges: A Resource Guide for Tribal/County Intergovernmental Cooperation* (Seattle: Northwest Renewable Resources Center, 1997).

Keith C. Petersen, *River of Life, Channel of Death: Fish and Dams on the Lower Snake* (Lewiston, ID: Confluence Press, 1995).

Earl Pomeroy, *The Pacific Slope: A History of California, Oregon, Washington, Idaho, Utah, & Nevada* (Seattle: University of Washington Press, 1965).

Kent D. Richards, *Isaac I. Stevens: Young Man in a Hurry* (Provo, UT: Brigham Young University Press, 1979).

Judith Roche and Meg McHutchison, eds., *First Fish, First People: Salmon Tales of the North Pacific Rim* (Seattle: University of Washington Press, 1998).

Roger Sale, *Seattle: Past to Present* (Seattle: University of Washington Press, 1976).

Paul Chaat Smith and Robert Allen Warrior, *Like a Hurricane: The Indian Movement from Alcatraz to Wounded Knee* (New York: New Press, 1996).

Wallace Stegner, *Wolf Willow: A History, a Story, and a Memory of the Last Plains Frontier* (New York: Viking Press, 1955).

Jacqueline M. Storm et al., *Land of the Quinault*, edited by Pauline K. Capoeman (Taholah, WA: Quinault Indian Nation, 1990).

James G. Swan, *The Northwest Coast: Three Years Residence in Washington Territory* (Seattle: University of Washington Press, 1982 ed.).

Edwin Way Teale, *The Wilderness World of John Muir* (Boston: Houghton Mifflin Co., 1954).

Richard White, *"It's Your Misfortune and None of My Own:" A New History of the American West* (Norman: University of Oklahoma Press, 1991).

———, *The Organic Machine* (New York: Hill & Wang, 1995).

Charles F. Wilkinson, *American Indians, Time, and the Law: Native Societies in a Modern Constitutional Democracy* (New Haven, CT: Yale University Press, 1987).

———, *Crossing the Next Meridian: Land, Water, and the Future of the West* (Washington, DC: Island Press, 1992).

———, *The Eagle Bird: Mapping a New West*, rev. ed. (Boulder, CO: Johnson Books, 1999).

Edward O. Wilson, *The Diversity of Life* (New York: W.W. Norton & Co., 1992).

ARTICLES

Thomas F. Haensly, "Equitable Apportionment of Intertribal Shares of Anadromous Fish," vol. 8, *Stanford Environmental Law Journal*, pp. 174–99 (1989).

"Indian War in Washington Territory: Special Agent W.B. Gosnell's Report in 1856," vol. 17, *Washington Historical Quarterly*, pp. 289–99 (1926).

Thomas C. Jensen, "The United States–Canada Pacific Salmon Interception Treaty: An Historical and Legal Overview," vol. 16, *Environmental Law*, pp. 363–422 (1986).

Ralph W. Johnson, "Regulation of Commercial Salmon Fishermen: A Case of Confused Objectives," vol. 55, *Pacific Northwest Quarterly*, pp. 141–45 (1964).

———, "The States Versus Indian Off-Reservation Fishing: A United States Supreme Court Error," vol. 47, *Washington Law Review*, pp. 207–36 (1972).

———, "Fragile Gains: Two Centuries of Canadian and United States Policy Toward Indians," vol. 66, *Washington Law Review*, pp. 643–718 (1991).

"Letters of Governor Isaac I. Stevens, 1853-1854," vol. 30, *Pacific Northwest Quarterly*, pp. 301–37 (1939).

William D. Newmark, "A Land-Bridge Island Perspective on Mammalian Extinctions in Western North American Parks," vol. 325, *Nature*, pp. 430–32 (1987).

———, "Extinction of Mammal Populations in Western North American National Parks," vol. 9, *Conservation Biology*, pp. 512–26 (1995).

Northwest Indian Fisheries Commission, "Tribes Applaud ESA Secretarial Order," vol. 2, *Northwest Indian Fisheries Commission News*, p. 8 (1997).

Reed F. Noss et al., "Conservation Biology and Carnivore Conservation in the Rocky Mountains," vol. 10, *Conservation Biology*, pp. 949–63 (1996).

Laurie Reynolds, "Indian Hunting and Fishing Rights: The Role of Tribal Sovereignty and Preemption," vol. 62, *North Carolina Law Review*, pp. 743–93 (1984).

Rod Vessels, "Treaties: Fishing Rights in the Pacific Northwest — The Supreme Court 'Legislates' an Equitable Solution," vol. 8, *American Indian Law Review*, pp. 117–37 (1980).

Charles F. Wilkinson and Daniel Keith Conner, "The Law of the Pacific Salmon Fishery: Conservation and Allocation of a Transboundary Common Property Resource," vol. 32, *Kansas Law Review*, pp. 17–109 (1983).

NEWSPAPER ARTICLES

Hank Adams, "Fishing: From Treaty to Treachery," *Renegade* (Franks Landing/Lacey, WA) (June 1972).

Ross Anderson, "River Watch: Divided Interests Make a Deal," *Seattle Times/Seattle Post-Intelligencer* (May 17, 1987).

Paul Andrews, "Latest Boldt Decision a Shocker," *Seattle Times* (Feb. 8, 1979).

——— , "Boldt Out, but His Legacy Will Linger," *Seattle Times* (Feb. 8, 1979).

John Bailey, "Wa-He-Lut: Ancient Tree of Red Roots," *News Tribune* (Puget Sound, WA) (Oct. 1, 1977).

"Boldt Remembered," *Herald Republic* (Yakima, WA) (Mar. 22, 1984).

Earl Caldwell, "High Court Building Stormed in Demonstration by the Poor," *New York Times* (May 30, 1968).

Rob Carson, "Frank Approach: 'Renegade' Wins Prize for Humanitarianism," *News Tribune* (Puget Sound, WA) (May 25, 1992).

Peter Collier, "Salmon Fishing in America: The Indians vs. the State of Washington," *Renegade* (Franks Landing/Lacey, WA) (June 1971).

Mike Conant, "Indians Net New Troubles," *Daily Olympian* (WA) (Mar. 4, 1964).

John de Young, "Boldt's Good Deeds Will Live After Him," *Seattle Post-Intelligencer* (Mar. 21, 1984).

John Dodge, "Common Cause Honors Nisqually Activist Billy Frank for Coalition Work," *Olympian* (WA) (May 12, 1985).

Timothy Egan, "Indians and Salmon: Making Nature Whole," *New York Times*, (Nov. 26, 1992).

Mike Fitzgibbon, "Nisquallys, Army Hail New Fish Hatchery," *News Tribune* (Puget Sound, WA) (Aug. 18, 1991).

Susan Gordon, "Nisqually Tribe, City Settle Suit Over Dams," *News Tribune* (Puget Sound, WA) (May 25, 1989).

Don Hannula, "Blood Flows in Indian River Fight," *News Tribune* (Puget Sound, WA) (Oct. 14, 1965).

——— , "Hank Adams: Dedicated to His People's Fight for Rights," *Daily Olympian* (WA) (Jan. 19, 1971).

——— , "State Stealing Nets Since 1960s, Indian Tells Trial," *Seattle Times* (Sept. 11, 1973).

——— , "Popularity Not Factor in Fishing Case for Judge," *Seattle Times* (Mar. 19, 1974).

——— , "Bill Frank's Long Journey," *Seattle Times* (May 10, 1985).

A. Richard Immel, "In Washington State Indians, White Men Battle Over Fish," *Wall Street Journal* (Mar. 1, 1978).

"Indians Join Throng at Service for Boldt," *Seattle Post-Intelligencer* (Mar. 25, 1984).

"Indians Win Fish Case," *Columbian* (Vancouver, BC) (Feb. 12, 1974).

Bruce Johnson, "Nisquallys Warn They May Arm," *News Tribune* (Puget Sound, WA) (Oct. 10, 1965).

"Judge Boldt Left His Mark," *Olympian* (WA) (Mar. 20, 1984).

Mike Layton, "Gregory Makes Bail to Join a St. Martin's Fish-In Panel," *Daily Olympian* (WA) (Feb. 17, 1966).

"The Legacy of Boldt: History Will Treat Him More Kindly," *Seattle Times* (Mar. 20, 1984).

Jack Mayne, "Fishing Rights Judge Raps Court No-Shows," *Seattle Post-Intelligencer* (Mar. 19, 1974).

———, "Indians Hold State Cannot Bar Fishing," *Seattle Post-Intelligencer* (Dec. 11, 1973).

Dick Monaghan, "Nisqually War Quiets Down to Cease Fire," *News Tribune* (Puget Sound, WA) (Jan. 10, 1962).

Bob Mottram, "Task Force to Recommend Opening Shores to Logging," *News Tribune* (Puget Sound, WA) (Mar. 13, 1983).

Sylvia Wieland Nogaki, "End Fishing Conflict, Activist Asks" *Seattle Times/Seattle Post-Intelligencer* (Oct. 18, 1992).

Laura Parker, "Angling for Time to Save the Salmon" *Seattle Post-Intelligencer* (Dec 12, 1982).

Elaine Porterfield, "Cooperation a Necessity, Indian Leader Frank Says," *News Tribune* (Puget Sound, WA) (Oct. 18, 1992).

Eric Pryne, "Big Business Enters Indian-Fishing Issue," *Seattle Times* (May 8,1981).

Eric Pryne and Dick Lilly, "Indian Leader Gets Coveted Honor," *Seattle Times* (May 25, 1992).

Jamie Sanchez, "The Nisqually Indian Reservation," *Renegade* (Franks Landing/ Lacey, WA) (June 1972).

Bruce Sherman, "Friends & Foes Mourn Judge Boldt, Dead at 80," *Seattle Post-Intelligencer* (Mar. 20, 1984).

Paul E. Steiger, "Pay Board Chairman Noted for Fairness," *Los Angeles Times* (Oct. 26, 1971).

Brooks Townes, "Dick Gregory Drops a Net: Fish-In Forces Capture a
    Comic," *Olympian* (WA) (Feb. 7, 1966).
Jeff Weathersby, "Timber, Fisheries Interests Walking New Path," *News
    Tribune* (Puget Sound, WA) (Dec. 27, 1987).
Jack Wilkins, "Court to Hear Voice from Past," *News Tribune* (Tacoma) (Aug.
    31, 1973).
———, "Judge Boldt Says Purpose of Reservations Key Question in Case,"
    News Tribune (Tacoma) (Sept. 7, 1973).
———, "Indian, 86, Recalls Fishing Fun of Past," *News Tribune* (Tacoma)
    (Sept. 12, 1973).
Rusty Yerxa, "Fish-In: No Arrests Planned," *Seattle Times* (Jan. 25, 1973).

GOVERNMENT PUBLICATIONS AND OTHER DOCUMENTS

Susan Amberson et al., "The Delta Plan" (Olympia, WA: Nisqually. . . . The
    Delta Project, n.d.).
Cherokee Nation v. Georgia, 30 U.S. (5 Pet.) 1 (1831).
City of Centralia, Washington, 29 F.E.R.C. ¶ 61,295 (1984).
City of Tacoma, Washington, 62 F.E.R.C. ¶ 63,032 (1993).
"Compilation of Major Post-Trial Orders Through June 30, 1978," *United
    States v. Washington*, 459 F.Supp. 1020 (W.D.Wash.1978).
Consoer, Townsend and Associates, "Nisqually River Basin Water Quality
    Management Plan" (Tacoma, WA: n.p., 1974).
Department of Game v. Puyallup Tribe (Puyallup II), 414 U.S. 44 (1973).
Deposition of Bill Frank, Jr., June 12, 1973, in the District Court of the United
    States for the Western District of Washington at Tacoma, *United States v.
    Washington* (Boldt decision), 384 F.Supp. 312 (W.D.Wash.1974).
George Gibbs, "Record of the Proceedings of the Commission to Hold
    Treaties with the Indian Tribes in Washington Territory and the Blackfoot
    Country" (Records of the Washington Superintendent of Indian Affairs,
    Dec. 7, 1854 – Mar. 3, 1855).
Johnson v. McIntosh, 21 U.S. (8 Wheat.) 543 (1823).
Chris Maun, "The Living River: A Guide to the Nisqually River Basin"
    (Yelm, WA: Nisqually River Education Project, 1996).
Nisqually River Task Force and Washington Department of Ecology,

"Nisqually River Management Plan: Final Environmental Impact Statement" (Washington State Department of Ecology, 1987).

Northwest Indian Fisheries Commission, AComprehensive Tribal Natural Resource Management: A Report from the Treaty Indian Tribes in Western Washington, 1997" (Olympia, WA: Northwest Indian Fisheries Commission, 1997).

Plaintiffs' Post-Trial Brief, Oct. 31, 1973, in the District Court of the United States for the Western District of Washington at Tacoma, *United States v. Washington*, 384 F.Supp. 312 (W.D.Wash.1974) (No. 9213).

Puyallup Tribe v. Department of Game (Puyallup I), 391 U.S. 392 (1968).

Puyallup Tribe v. Department of Game (Puyallup III), 433 U.S. 165 (1977).

Sohappy v. Smith, 302 F.Supp. 899 (D.Or.1969).

State v. Towessnute, 89 Wash. 478, 154 P. 805 (1916).

Testimony of Bill Frank, Jr., Sept. 10, 1973, in the District Court of the United States for the Western District of Washington at Tacoma, *United States v. Washington*, 384 F.Supp. 312 (W.D.Wash.1974).

Treaty of Medicine Creek, 26 Dec. 1854 (ratified Mar. 3, 1855), U.S.–Nisqualli, Puyallup, Steilacoom, Squawskin, S'Homamish, Stehchass, T'Peeksin, Squi-aitl, and Sa-heh-wamish tribes and bands of Indians, available in Charles J. Kappler, *Laws & Treaties*, vol. 2, p. 661 (1904).

Tulee v. Washington, 315 U.S. 681 (1942).

United States v. Washington (Boldt decision), 384 F.Supp. 312 (W.D.Wash.1974).

United States v. Winans, 198 U.S. 371 (1905).

Washington v. Washington State Commercial Passenger Fishing Vessel Association, 443 U.S. 658 (1979).

Winters v. United States, 207 U.S. 564 (1908).

Worcester v. Georgia, 31 U.S. (6 Pet.) 515 (1832).

VIDEOS

In the Shadow of the Eagle, produced by Jenö Farkas, Arne Ullum, and Lee McLaren (Nomad Film, 1991).

The North American Indian, Part 1: Treaties Made, Treaties Broken, produced and directed by Ross Devenish (McGraw-Hill Contemporary Films, 1970).

CREDITS

Salmon glyph reproduced from a carving by **Alex Jackson**, Tlingit artist
Maps (endsheets and pp. 24 and 70) by **Diane Sylvain**
Cartoon (p. 92) by **David Horsey**. Copyright (1991) *Seattle Post-Intelligencer*

PHOTOGRAPH COLLECTIONS

Permission for use of photographs courtesy of: The **Maiselle Bridges** family
collection, Frank's Landing, pp. 5, 6, 25, 33, 35, 37, 39, 40, 42, 44, 45, 97, 102;
CurrentRutledge, Ltd. (Seattle), 33, 65, 102; **Nisqually Indian Tribe**, 8, 9, 13,
22; **Northwest Indian Fisheries Commission**, 48 (1965), 57 (1982), 60 (left)
(1978), 67; **Puyallup Tribal News**, 97; **Special Collections Division**, University
of Washington Libraries, 13 (FM-25, Neg. No. NA709), 22 (FM-25, Neg. No.
NA1225; Meany Collection No. 42); **Survival of American Indians Association** [from brochure], 47; **Thames Television** (London), 6 (1969); **Upstream
Productions** (Seattle), 60, 61 (1996); **Wa He Lut Indian School** [State Centen-
nial], vi (1989); **Washington State Department of Fisheries**, 86-87 [in Arthur
R. Kruckeberg, *A Natural History of Puget Sound Country*, University of
Washington Press (1991), 283]; **Washington State Historical Society**, 8, 9
[Washington Capitol Museum], 10, 12 [in Ezra Meeker, *The Tragedy of Leschi*
(1905), republished with new materials by the Historical Society of Seattle and
King County, Museum of History and Industry (1980)]

PHOTOGRAPHERS

Hank Adams, pp. 55 (1989), 59 (1988), 79 (1991), 83 (1999), 95 (1995), 96
(1998), 98 (1999); **Elmer Allen**, 33 (n.d.), 39 (1969), 44 (1970), 45 (1968);
Tom Brownell, 63 (March 9, 1970). Courtesy of *Seattle Post-Intelligencer*;
Dan Budnick, 35 [in Robert McLaughlin, "The Native American Challenge:
In Pursuit of Tribal Sovereignty," *Juris Doctor*, October 1976]; **Carol Burns**,
64 (left) (1969). Courtesy of Alison Gottfriedson; **Greg Gilbert**, 50 (February

BRITI
VANCOUVER ISLAND
Lummi
STRAIT OF JUAN DE FUCA
Makah
Lower Elwha
Quileute
Hoh
Quinault
Jamestown
Port Gamble
OLYMPIC NATIONAL PARK
Suquamish
PACIFIC OCEAN
Skokomish
Squaxin Island
0 10 20
miles
Olympia
Frank's Landing